Corvette C5

Mike Mueller

MBI Publishing Company

First published in 1998 by MBI Publishing Company, 729 Prospect Avenue, PO Box 1, Osceola, WI 54020-0001 USA.

The information in this book is true and complete to the best of our knowledge. All recommendations are made without any guarantee on the part of the author or Publisher, who also disclaim any liability incurred in connection with the use of this data or specific details.

We recognize that some words, model names, and designations, for example, mentioned herein are the property of the trademark holder. We use them for identification purposes only. This is not an official publication.

MBI Publishing Company books are also available at discounts in bulk quantity for industrial or sales-promotional use. For details write to Special Sales Manager at Motorbooks International Wholesalers & Distributors, 729 Prospect Avenue, Osceola, WI 54020-0001 USA.

Library of Congress Cataloging-in-Publication Data

Mueller, Mike.
    Corvette C5 / Mike Mueller.
       p. cm. – (ColorTech series)
    Includes index.
    ISBN 0-7603-0457-2 (pbk. : alk. paper)
    1. Corvette automobile. I. Title. II. Series.
    TL215.C6M8398 1998   98-16421
    629.222'2–dc21

On the front cover: After about eight years of development work, the all-new C5 finally debuted in Detroit in January 1997. This 1997 coupe features the optional bodyside protective strip. It is owned by Kelly Sellers of Champaign, Illinois. *Mike Mueller*

On the frontispiece: This rendering shows much of the final C5 form; the "double-bubble" roof, the hoods subtle contours, the bodyside scallops. Wind tunnel demands, as well as subjective opinions, probably ruled out this attractive nose, which does appear much more distinctive than the final result. *Copyright 1996 GM Corp. Used with permission GM Media Archives.*

On the titlepage: The ghost view shows just how much the tightly packaged chassis layout helped give the C5 convertible so much storage space. And with the top up, this car still manages a 0.32 drag coefficient, only 0.03 less than the wind-cheating coupe. *courtesy Chevrolet Motor Division, GM Corporation*

On the back cover: The Corvette became a two-model family again in 1998 with the convertible's return. A third model, a first for America's sports car, is scheduled to appear soon. The red 1997 coupe belongs to Mike and Sandy Duncan of Buford, Georgia. *Mike Mueller*

Edited by Anne McKenna
Designed by Katie L. Sonmor

Printed in China through World Print, Ltd.

CONTENTS

The photo work for this book may have never gotten off the ground if it wasn't for the cooperation and patience of Tom and Kelly Sellers of Champaign, Illinois. Kelly's 1997 C5 coupe did a great job, too.

ACKNOWLEDGMENTS

I tend to be a lucky guy, even more so now that I rushed off that chain letter to five of my soon-to-be-not-so-close friends. Come on, guys, it said it right there in black and white, "break the chain, and great doom and gloom will surely be yours." Don't say I didn't warn you.

Back to the subject at hand.

That subject is Corvettes. And not just any Corvettes, the best 'Vettes yet, the all-new, all-powerful C5 models—the ground-breaking coupe and reaffirming convertible. I was lucky enough (there it is again) to have MBI Publishing ask me to drop my doughnut and hammer out yet another epic, this one, of course, about the C5, the greatest Corvette to come along since . . . well, since man first walked upright and started looking for a way to upstage his neighbor by parking something really hot out in front of the cave.

Of course, there's more to Corvette ownership than that, although it certainly doesn't hurt to have a spare one around at parties. Me, I only get to write about them. And

photograph them. And drive 'em now and again. And have a great time doing all of the above.

Isn't that what owning a Corvette is all about? Enjoying life. Having fun behind the wheel. Let everyone else get from point A to point B. In a Corvette, that trip is never a straight line. Nor is it for everyone. If practical transportation is the only thought that comes to mind whenever automobiles are mentioned, you can stop reading right now and go back to your rice cake.

As for me, I love driving. And I've always loved Corvettes, dating back to the day when I took delivery of a pedal-powered model at age two. I still regret trading that baby in on a Radio Flyer.

Even though I don't own one today, I still have more than my share of fun with Corvettes. When this opportunity came up, all I could utter was, "Is this a great country or what?" To say I enjoyed putting this project together goes without saying. So I won't.

Well-known Corvette enthusiast Ray Quinlan, of Champaign, Illinois, was an immense help to the author on this project. Here, Quinlan beams in September 1994 next to the 1953 Corvette he donated to the National Corvette Museum in Bowling Green, Kentucky. At the time, he was on hand to mark the NCM's grand opening.

But I will say how much fun it was to meet the people, the owners, and the other folks out there who also enjoy Corvettes right down to the bone. It was these people who made writing and photographing this book an adventure, not a job. I can't possibly pay you all back for your efforts. So I won't.

What I might do is thank you all heartily and promise to pick up the tab (once more) the next time I'm in town.

First and foremost, this book owes so much to Tom Sellers and his new wife Kelly, who was his girlfriend in 1997 when the four of us—Tom, Kelly, I, and Kelly's 1997 coupe—spent the better part of a week together in Champaign, Illinois. Tom and Kelly bent over backwards during those hot days to allow me to shoot the Corvette inside and out, then worked overtime at night running up the finance charge on my Visa card. Thanks a lot, guys.

Seriously, though, I could certainly do a lot worse for friends. And I'm sure you two feel the same way about me. Many happy years together, you nuts.

Along with Tom and Kelly, the ever-present Ray Quinlan was also always on hand in Champaign to help out, as he has been every year since we first hooked up back in my college days at the University of Illinois. Where have those 15 years gone? Ray, one of the greatest fiberglass fanatics I know, dropped everything repeatedly to help point me in the right direction. And he also opened up his shop, Quality Auto Care, for my use. Special thanks go to Ray's daughter, Peggy Ishcomer, and ace mechanics Dan Tharp, Bob Lance, and Phil Berger for their patience and kind assistance while I had Kelly's Corvette up on a lift photographing the dirty side. Next time, Kelly, would you scrub that area with a toothbrush, too?

Another Corvette crazy and a good friend that I might never have met if it weren't for Ray Quinlan again pointing the way, Bill Tower of Plant City, Florida, worked similar wonders down in the Sunshine State. He was busy arranging C5 photo shoots even when I wasn't around to trip the trigger. He even dusted off his 1975 Sting Ray convertible for a quick session with Tom Riley's red 1997 coupe, that coming on the same day he also rolled out (literally, we didn't dare start it) his fabulous 1967 L88 for a quick shoot at sunset. Big thanks go to Bill and Tom, the latter of Clearwater, Florida.

A mutual friend of Bill's and mine, *Road & Track* photographer Bill Warner, was more than willing to uncover his 1954 Corvette for some lens time with a blue 1998 convertible. As always, whenever Mr. Warner's around, a good time was had by all.

Back in Champaign, I owe a debt of gratitude to Elmer Lash (yet again) for pulling out his incredible 1961 big-tank fuelie for 15 minutes of fame in front of my Hasselblad. Champaign's Bob Wolter, too. Bob actually loaned his red 1967 Sting Ray to me sight unseen. Equally cooperative were Mike and Sandy Duncan and Richard Corwin. The

Duncans, from Buford, Georgia, rolled out their red 1997 coupe for the camera. Corwin, of Snellville, Georgia, made his 1994 convertible available. Thanks, folks.

I must also thank my brother Jim Mueller, Jr. I must because he'll pout for a year if I don't. Jim has helped arrange many shoots over the years in the Champaign area, the latest involving the Sellers' C5 and Al Mitchell's white 1996 coupe. Jim's son Teddy was also recruited as a photo assistant and just might make a good photographer some day, as soon as I teach him how to throw a stepladder across a field in frustration. Hang time's the key, Ted. Hang time I say.

Also of great help was my brother-in-law, Frank Young, and his boy Jason, they too of Champaign. Jason has already got the ladder thing down. As for Frank, he's so good now he has the next film roll ready long before I get the chance to scream his name. I hope you know, Frank, you're taking all the fun out of stressing.

Then again, why stress when so many were willing to do so much for so little?

There's fellow Corvette authors Randy Leffingwell and Noland Adams in California. You guys didn't really do anything for me, but you did return my phone calls, which makes you A-okay in my book. Besides, Noland has been such a great help in the past. Randy, I'm still waiting on you, but you'll get your chance.

Others who also returned my calls were *Sports Car International*'s D. Randy Riggs, *Motor Trend*'s C. Van Tune, *Corvette Fever*'s Paul Zazarine (more than once, and at home to boot), *AutoWeek*'s Dutch Mandel, and Corvette Brand Manager Richard Almond. Wes Raynal at *Corvette Quarterly* might have called back one day if I had ever given him the chance. Thanks for talking, all of you.

And thanks for the pictures, all of them. From ace photographer Tom Glatch. From spy photographer Jim Dunne and his cohort in crime, Nick Twork. From Denise Kochis and Karen Spern at GM Archives. From Jeff Tate and Marc Lathan at Chevrolet Communications. From Paul Zazarine and Richard Newton at *Corvette Fever*. From artists Duane Kuchar and Joyce Tucker.

Joyce also deserves a handshake or two for being such a great right-hand woman. Her contribution to this book cannot be measured, no matter how you slice it. She supplied a conceptual sketch of the 1999 fixed-roof coupe. She wrote a sidebar on her good friend Jim Dunne. She made countless phone calls running down leads and stuff. She grabbed her own 15 minutes when I needed a model. Three times. And she hustled her hump off on photo shoot after photo shoot. All this without one complaint. Without one mention of remuneration. Without one threat of getting paybacks some day. So much for so little. How do you do it?

Last, but by no means least, special thanks go to Karan Howard of Marietta, Georgia, and Leslie Mathis of Lakeland, Florida. Both did a great job making cameo appearances on these pages. But did you have to upstage the cars? The checks are in the mail, ladies. When you get 'em, go crazy, as will I now that this deadline has finally been deep-sixed.

A special thanks has to go to these special assistants who made so many photo opportunities possible. From left to right: Illinois State Police Master Sergeant Frank Young (the author's brother-in-law) and his son Jason; Teddy Mueller and his father Jim Mueller Jr. (the author's little brother). *Nancy Mueller*

INTRODUCTION
THE BEST 'VETTE YET

Motor Trend's editors have been dishing out their coveted "Car of the Year" honors almost uninterrupted since 1949, the exceptions being 1950 and 1953–1955. Up through 1997, 45 Car of the Year awards have gone to a wide array of automobiles, from the compact Rambler, to the enigmatic Citroën SM, to the luxurious Lincoln Town Car. Special categories also have been created over the years, first for imports and, more recently, for the rapidly growing wave of pickup trucks and sport utilities now flooding the market.

All told, Chevrolet has snatched up 11 of those awards, beginning with the controversial Corvair in 1960. Lately, General Motors' price leader has been especially good in the eyes of *MT*'s staff. Up through 1997, Chevrolet products had copped *Motor Trend's* "Golden Calipers" trophy for three straight years, with Blazer, the division's compact SUV, starting the string as Truck of the Year in 1995. Tahoe, Chevrolet's full-sized sport-ute, repeated that honor in 1996. And Chevy's reborn Malibu midsized sedan was Car of the Year in 1997.

That, however, was then. What about now? What has Chevy done for us lately?

That question has been answered once more by *Motor Trend* this year with yet another Car of the Year award. The winner? Making it four straight for Chevrolet is none other than the all-new, fifth-generation Corvette, the groundbreaking, head-turning, blood-pumping, all-American sports car that had first went on sale in targa-top form in January

---

Can you believe it? Chevrolet's Corvette is now 45 years old and looking better than ever. Times, tastes, and the cars themselves have certainly changed since America's sports car was born in 1953. In 1998 a convertible returned to the two-seat line-up after a one-year hiatus.

Corvette's first generation, we may now all call it "C1," ran from 1953 to 1962 and encompassed the "solid-axle" years. Shown here with a 1997 C5 coupe is a 1961 fuel-injected Corvette with the optional removable hardtop.

1997 (too late to meet *Motor Trend*'s eligibility deadline for 1996); it was then joined by a certifiably sexy, topless running mate for 1998. Chevrolet calls it the "C5." *Motor Trend*'s judge and jury preferred a few more words, labeling it "the most significant new car of the year, the one vehicle that packs the greatest importance in terms of technological advancement, overall value, driving character, performance, functional abilities, and market impact."

No, the C5 didn't win just because of its fast and furious nature. And yes, Petersen Publishing's people could simply let their rapid heartbeats determine their decisions, giving their annual award to only the hottest cars out there. But the C5 won both because *Motor Trend* staffers do check their hearts at the door and because the car itself did meet all the above criteria. Impressively. As planned. From Chief Engineer David Hill on down, everyone involved in the new Corvette's design recognized that world-class horsepower and handling alone wouldn't do if the C5 was truly meant to be a world-class sports car, an American world-class sports car.

"While speed and acceleration are important," explained John Heinricy, director of Corvette total vehicle integration, "customers preferred a balanced car that handled the rigors of everyday driving exceptionally well, not one strictly oriented toward straight-line speed."

"We designed the car with a synchronous mindset," added Interior Designer Jon Albert. "We focused on individual goals, such as improved performance, reduced mass, and increased reliability, within the overall framework of the whole car. We evaluated and balanced each change so as to optimize the total car."

Indeed, the C5 Corvette is a "total car," or at least as total a car as a two-seat, 180-mile-per-hour performance machine can get at the price. Wearing what can be

Electronic fuel injection has been a Corvette standard since 1985. But "fuelie" 'Vettes are certainly nothing new. A mechanical F.I. option debuted in 1957. Here, the Corvette's first chief engineer, Zora Duntov (right), looks over the new performance equipment in 1957 with legendary automotive journalist Tom McCahill. *Courtesy Chevrolet and Noland Adams*

considered an affordable (for a world-class sports car) price tag that falls just short of $40,000, the C5 does rank as the fastest street-legal automobile for the dollar available in this country. Beyond that, the fifth-generation Corvette offers more of so much more. More comfort. More convenience. More cool. More car.

"The [new] Corvette is the Super Bowl of design projects," said Chief Designer John Cafaro. "We knew this would be the greatest sports car ever done. Bar none."

Forget, for a moment, Cafaro's stunning new styling, which not only looks fabulous but also cuts

The first Sting Rays, or "midyear" models, made up the second generation, which ran for five years only, 1963 to 1967. This midyear is a 1967 coupe with optional knock-off wheels and side-mount exhausts.

through the wind unlike anything else ever to escape from Detroit. Beneath that slippery skin is a proliferous proliferation of design and technology tricks intended to enhance every facet of the car's reinvented brand of performance. The innovative frame with its rigid central tunnel and hydroformed perimeter rails made the car 4.5 times stiffer than the C4 platform. This extra rigidity helped improve both handling and ride and did away with many of the squeaky gremlins inherent in earlier Corvettes, a constant complaint that C5 designers all knew needed major attention.

Additional shakes, rattles, and rolls were sought out and eliminated by reducing total components by a third, amounting to an amazing 1,500 parts that the C4 had and the C5 doesn't. This reduction also simplified production and maintenance. As Corvette Quality Engineering Manager Rod Michaelson explained, "the 1,500 parts eliminated equates to 1,500 opportunities for something to go wrong that aren't there any more."

Another boost to ride and handling came by way of the rear-mounted transmission. This long-discussed idea not only helped bring the car's weight distribution closer

A headline-making, all-new Corvette is also nothing new. In 1963, the redesigned Sting Ray woke everyone up. Among its various engineering innovations was a "birdcage" structure beneath the new coupe's bodyshell to help solidify the platform. Sound familiar? *Courtesy Chevrolet and Noland Adams*

Corvette's third generation lived the longest, making 15 model-year appearances from 1968 to 1982. Taking a time-out with this red 1997 coupe is a 1975 Sting Ray convertible. The optional removable roof is in place.

Once the C4 Corvette did finally appear in March 1983, its updates were lauded highly by the press. Although not quite what you'd call a backbone chassis, the new C4's underbody equipment included a spine that tied together the transmission in front and the differential housing in back. *Courtesy Corvette Fever, Dobbs Publishing Group*

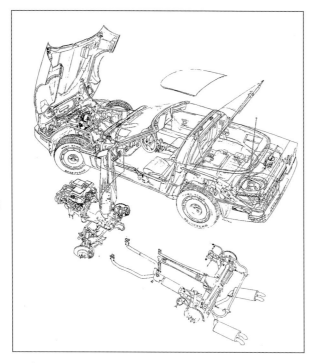

to the preferred performance-conscious 50/50 front/rear balance, it also freed up space beneath the passenger compartment, meaning both driver and passenger now have more room down there in the footwells to stretch out and ride comfortably. The entire compartment itself is roomier thanks to the fact that all four wheels have been moved farther out to the corners.

And those stronger hydroformed frame rails also allowed the Corvette's typically high door sill to be dropped down 3.7 inches, a change warmly welcomed by long-legged, short-skirted drivers. Eagle-eyed, single-minded bystanders who have long taken advantage of the unintended view as these women tried vainly to enter or exit an earlier Corvette in lady-like fashion are now spit out of luck. You guys can all now turn your attention to those too-tall SUVs.

Not to be overlooked, the C5's LS1 powerplant is equally newsworthy, although it does remain tied, like its

LT1 and LT4 predecessors, to age-old pushrod, two-valve technology. Simplicity was among the goals here. Why complicate production and installation and increase costs by using overhead cams and four-valve heads—especially when a more traditional V-8 could still supply ample power to keep the fiberglass faithful happy?

The C5's 345-horsepower Gen III V-8 still features the same "440" cylinder block structure (it measures 4.4 inches from bore center to bore center) and 5.7-liter displacement figure shared by previous Chevy small-blocks. "After all," said LS1 Engine Program Manager John Juriga, "some things are sacred." From there, it's an entirely new breed. Most notably, the LS1 is Chevrolet's first all-aluminum, regular-production small-block. It's both lighter and more durable than the C4's 5.7L V-8.

The list continues. Brakes, tires, suspension—not one stone was left unturned while making the C5 into a supreme sports car.

"The fifth-generation Corvette is a refined Corvette, in all the right ways," said David Hill. "We examined our weak points and turned them into strengths. Things that were good, we made great. Things that were great are now even better."

More specifically, the C5 is now every bit as much car as it is sports car. "It's more user-friendly," continued Hill. "It's easier to get in and out of, and it's more ergonomic. It has greater visibility; it's more comfortable and more functional. It provides more sports car for the money than anything in its market segment. It'll pull nearly 1g, and it starts and stops quicker than you can blink."

The C5 has not only demonstrated just how good a Corvette can get, it also has reminded customers that the heartbeat still goes on for the Bow-Tie boys. "Winning a fourth consecutive *Motor Trend* award proves that the Chevrolet product renaissance is continuing at full throttle," said division General Manager John G. Middlebrook, who knows full well the value of the fiberglass legacy. "Corvette is now, and will continue to remain, Chevrolet's flagship," he continued. "It is our technological and image showcase. Even more importantly, Corvette stands as the most singularly dramatic example of what we mean by 'Genuine Chevrolet.'"

Hands down, the C5 is clearly the most significant new car of 1998. And with due respect to so many other great 'glass two-seaters of the past, it easily stands as the most noteworthy Corvette yet. Just Car of the Year? Come on now.

Corvette was simply Car of the Year in 1984, and rightly so. Chevrolet's first C4, of course, ranks as a model-line milestone and did show off an updated chassis. The long-awaited 1984 Corvette was certainly award-worthy, but it left the sports car crowd stirred, not shaken. The C5, on the other hand, has rocked our world. "It will be remembered as one of the greatest cars in American automotive history," claimed *Motor Trend* when announcing the 1998 Corvette as its 46th Car of the Year. Should that then have been something more appropriate, say, like Car of the Millennium? Though that might be stretching things (just a bit), any way you look at it, you've got to give this world-class performance machine credit. How much is your prerogative.

Most journalists have gushed like Old Faithful stuck on fast forward. "If, as they say, God is in the details, then this is the first holy Corvette," wrote *Car and Driver*'s Csaba Csere. According to *Automobile* head honcho David E. Davis, Jr., "the '97 Corvette C5 is a home run in every way." "Like no Corvette before," added a *Road & Track* report, "[the C5] now possesses the sort of smoothness and refinement that, if it were a Scotch, could only be attributed to decades of little lessons learned about distillation and years of quiet aging."

Okay.

Of course Chevrolet people have also been more than willing to do a little (or a lot of) gushing on their own. David Hill got right to the point, describing the C5 as "the best 'Vette yet." Continued Hill, "you won't find a car in Corvette's price range that provides the same level of quality, power, ride, handling, and refinement. The fifth generation is the best in many, many ways." Is he biased? Naturally a tad. Then again, it ain't bragging if it's true.

Bowling Green, Kentucky, has been home to Corvette production since 1981. Previously, the car was built in St. Louis and briefly in Flint, Michigan, early in 1953. On July 2, 1992, the one-millionth Corvette—shown here with a 1953 model—rolled off the Bowling Green assembly line. Notice the sign: the Chevrolet-Pontiac-Canada group was dissolved not long after the millionth Corvette was built.

Second longest run in the Corvette legacy was the C4, born in 1984 after Chevrolet opted to skip the 1983 model year. In front of the 1998 C5 convertible is a 1994 C4 droptop.

But isn't it also true that "all-new" always qualifies as "best-yet" in Detroit? And couldn't this ever-present reality have unduly inspired so many worshippers down on their knees? Not the case here. If anything, the C5 has redefined all-new, certainly in Corvette terms, perhaps by all standards. The 1997 Corvette emerged as the first of its breed able to undeniably claim new-from-the-ground-up status. Even the original new Corvette in 1953 borrowed many of its components from Chevrolet's passenger-car parts shelf, which was then a very mundane place to shop. And not even the redesigned 1984 Corvette qualified; it may have featured a new body and state-of-the-art chassis, but its engine was the same Cross-Fire 350 small-block V-8 used by the previous generation.

A majority of C5 components were designed exclusively for the latest, greatest Corvette. And discounting a few fasteners and the modified 4L60-E automatic transmission (when installed in place of the six-speed manual), no parts were carried over from the C4. All-new, for once, truly means all-new.

Yet, at the risk of sounding contradictory, various aspects of the C5 follow in the everything-old-is-new-again tradition. Inside, the mildly double-humped dash mimics the design that welcomed Sting Ray buyers back in 1963. Even a passenger-side grab bar on the dash—a Corvette touch dating to 1956—is back in place, and it too is strongly reminiscent of the first Sting Ray.

On the outside, the C5 features, in Chevrolet's words, "new exterior styling that echoes the past and announces the future." While creating a look that will remain excitingly fresh well into the next millennium was a priority for John Cafaro's styling team, so too was the need to keep the new Corvettes looking at least a little something like the old Corvettes. All of them. Paying respect to a 45-year-old legacy was a major part of the job.

In 45 years the Corvette has had but three chief engineers. Zora Duntov (seated in the CERV III concept car) officially headed things from 1957 (he joined the Corvette team right after the car's 1953 debut) to 1975. Dave McLellan, at left, ruled from 1975 to 1992. David Hill, on right, has been in charge since. In between Hill and McLellan is former Chevrolet General Manager Jim Perkins. All four men were gathered together to mark the National Corvette Museum's grand opening during Labor Day weekend, September 1994. Duntov died at age 86 in 1996.

"We know our buyers," said Cafaro. "So while there was a whole list of areas we wanted to improve, we knew in our hearts that this Corvette had to be instantly recognizable as a Corvette." Thus, certain long-standing queues have either carried over or been added. The hardtop's lift-up "fastback" rear glass hearkens back to a 1978 beginning. The removable roof panel to 1968. The four taillights to 1961. The swooping bodyside coves to 1956. The C5 convertible's stylish seat-divider panel to 1953. A

WHAT A DIFFERENCE 40-SOMETHING YEARS MAKE

The years have certainly been kind to the Corvette. At 45, Chevrolet's fantastic plastic flight of fancy is still kicking tail and taking names and looking not a day over 16 while doing it. We should all be so lucky.

No other American fun-mobile can match the Corvette's longevity. None. Such a claim to fame would be big enough news even if you didn't consider this car's oh-so-narrow niche, its almost arrogant "I-don't-need-you, you-need-me" position in the marketplace. That customers have continued to grab up Corvettes as fast as they can be built for so long now is a testament both to this two-seater's intoxicating appeal and the basic nature of the American way. We're Yankees. We can indulge ourselves with such hedonism; it's our unalienable right. We don't actually need a car like the Corvette—we want it. We want it bad. And what we want, we buy, regardless of cost or how much it inflames our aging, aching backs. Is this a great country or what?

America was a great country too in 1952, only it didn't have its own sports car. What it did have was a bunch of little European two-seaters putting around, these introduced to our shores by scores of U.S. servicemen who had caught more than one bug while doing their duty in England during World War II. This particular affliction involved an uncontrollable desire to have fun behind the wheel of an automobile, to feel the wind in your hair, the bugs in your teeth, the rain down your neck, the tool pouch at arm's reach.

Living with a sports car then wasn't just an adventure, it was a job. Almost everything required special effort. Wrestling that big, upright, unassisted steering wheel. Winding out those little weak-kneed four-cylinders. Unfolding an often clumsy, sometimes useless soft-top. Snapping on pesky side curtains. Going bump in the night when the electrics gave out. It just didn't get any better.

Such was the case for the first Corvette, introduced in January 1953. Slapped together, albeit cleverly, from off-the-shelf parts and somewhat roughly hewn out of fiberglass, America's first sports car (please excuse us, Mercer, Stutz, Muntz, Nash-Healey, et al.) did its darndest to mimic the European way. No windows. No door handles. Only two seats.

Where it fell short involved what came between those seats. Chevy's first Corvette was packaged plain and simple, one way only: Polo White paint, red interior, six-cylinder power—and an automatic transmission. Everyone then knew that a sports car needed a stick. While Chevrolet's Blue Flame Six—a nicely enhanced powerplant wholly undeserving of the slings and arrows commonly delivered its way from a modern viewpoint—did a damn good job spurring the horses on, that pukey Powerglide, two speeds and all, was a major disappointment. It took a couple years and near cancellation to correct the situation.

Briefly offered along with Chevy's new 265 V-8 in 1955, a three-speed manual transmission became the only real choice for Corvette buyers in 1956, the

All Corvettes from 1953 to 1962 also had trunks, a feature that disappeared with the arrival of the all-new Sting Ray. A top C5 priority was bringing a trunk back; it reappeared on the 1998 convertible.

As much as it appears dated today, Chevrolet's first Corvette in 1953 (this is actually a 1954 model) came off every bit as exciting, if not more, as the new C5. From 1953 to 1962, all Corvettes were convertibles.

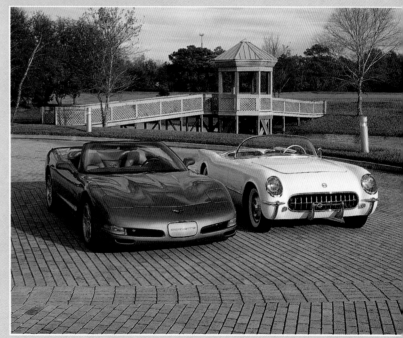

same year a fresh restyle brought along exterior door handles, roll-up windows, and an optional removable hardtop, all this in response to the plain truth that Yankees will be Yankees—we want it all. When "all" isn't available, "more" often suffices. So Chevrolet kept giving Corvette customers more. A four-speed and fuel injection in 1957. A coupe body, hideaway headlights, and independent rear suspension in 1963. Big-block V-8s and four-wheel disc brakes in 1965. A hatchback roof in 1978. Et cetera, et cetera.

With the dust clearing 45 years later, we now find ourselves with five, count 'em, five generations of Corvettes, each with its own decently distinctive place in history. And once Chevrolet told us all that the newest breed was identified in-house by the code C5, it then became only logical to retroactively label the entire progression accordingly. Thus, the original "solid-axle" cars built from 1953 to 1962 make up the C1 group. The midyear Sting Rays of 1963 to 1967 are now considered C2 models. The C3 years ran from 1968 to 1982 and the C4 years from 1984 to 1996. How long the C5 will roll on into the future is anyone's guess, although it's a fair bet it won't come anywhere close to the records set down by C3 and C4.

As much as Chevrolet officials like to talk about how much of those four previous generations still lives in the C5, there are critics out there who feel the new Corvette has actually lost touch with its roots.

"When you build on 40-plus years of heritage, you need to make some vestiges of that past apparent," said *Corvette Fever's* Paul Zazarine. "There are vestiges of the old Corvettes in there, but [Chevrolet people] have labored too hard to support this; they brag a little too much; they want to simply sell us on that idea."

Zazarine feels the new Corvette is "too refined." In his opinion, many of the quirks and "less comfortable" aspects addressed and corrected by the C5 redesign were among the things that helped endear the earlier generations of Corvettes to earlier generations of Corvette customers. "Yes, C4 was a compromise in many ways," he explained. "There were rattles and creaks, and it was hard to get in and out of, but that was all a part of the Corvette's charm, its persona, in the past. The C5 is a terrific car, but it lacks soul; it has lost its spirit, its true identity." And Zazarine is not alone in his beliefs. Even a former Chevrolet engineer has told him that "the new Corvette lacks visceral character."

On the other side of the coin you'll find all the raves. "The C5 Corvette effectively encapsulates 45 legendary years in a single benchmark vehicle that pushes the boundary of what a sports car could and should be, redefining the segment as both high-performance and functional," concluded *Motor Trend's* 1998 Car of the Year report. Whichever side of the

Early Corvette drivers were upright people. Notice the small floor shifter (all Corvettes from 1953 and 1954 were automatics) and the poorly located tachometer (the largest round gauge) in the center of the dash.

Comfort, convenience, and class are now all trademarks of the Corvette interior. Interior Designer Jon Albert's team left no stone unturned, no knob out of reach.

fence you stand on, there is one thing that can't be argued. Even Zazarine will admit the C5 is still a Corvette.

So was the 1990 ZR-1. The 1986 Indy Pace Car convertible. The 1970 LT-1. The 1963 Sting Ray. The 1957 "fuelie." And definitely the 1953. Sure, it looks dated today, what with its rippling, befinned bodywork, its skinny whitewalls, and those stone shields over its headlights. But the Corvette legacy had to start somewhere. Just remember, times do change, as do tastes, techno-trends, and government safety regulations. Long before people began jumping on the C5's bandwagon, they were waiting in line in the cold outside New York's Waldorf-Astoria hotel to get a peek at a dream machine the likes of which American car buyers had never seen before.

Some still haven't forgotten.

Corvette designers are especially proud of the C5 convertible's "waterfall," a seat divider that hearkens back to two-seaters of the past. That twin-fairing tonneau is also meant to remind onlookers of the car's great racing heritage.

The C5's seat divider was inspired by the first-generation Corvette. Shown here is a 1959 interior.

usable trunk, a long-since forgotten feature last found on a Corvette in 1962, was also added into the droptop equation for 1998.

Even the rear-mounted transmission is not entirely new; it was considered by Zora Duntov as early as 1957 for the "Q-Corvette" project, which many had hoped to see reach regular production in 1960. Although the innovative Q-Corvette didn't become a reality that year, the engine-in-front/transmission-in-back idea did see the light of day in Pontiac's Tempest in 1961.

Aluminum engine components also predate the C5 by almost four decades. Duntov briefly tried lightweight aluminum cylinder heads for the Corvette's solid-lifter 283 small-block in 1960 before production snafus derailed the plan. Seven years later, engineers introduced optional aluminum heads, RPO L89, for the 435-horse L71 427 big-block. They also unleashed the rare, race-only 1967 L88 Corvette with its unique, mean and nasty, aluminum-head 427. In 1969, Chevrolet even built two Corvettes with the ZL-1 427, another race-minded mill, this one of all-aluminum construction. On a more civilized note, aluminum heads were used atop the L98 350 small-block beginning in 1986.

So it is that the C5 both follows reverently in historic tire tracks and boldly takes off where no Corvette has gone before. And it has managed this feat seemingly against all odds. The car has earned all its honors and praises the old-fashioned way: it worked for it, and worked for it hard. Originally conceived in 1988 with hopes for an August 1992 introduction, just in time to serve as the Corvette's 40th anniversary 1993 model, the C5 was forced to endure an almost endless string of delayed decisions, budget crunches, personnel changes, personal battles, as well as all the other typical pitfalls automakers encounter when trying to design and build one of the greatest cars in automotive history.

Both planned debut dates and leading men came and went during the nearly nine-year trail from first sketches to the first C5 off the lot. Initial hopes called for the 1993

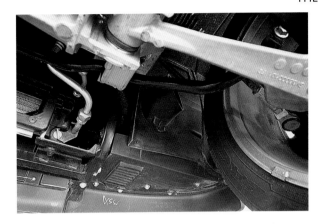

Among the countless innovative C5 chassis features is a small duct (to the left of tire, behind black stabilizer bar) at each front wheel that directs cooling air onto the disc-brake rotors.

Corvette engineers first tried the brake-cooling idea in 1957, offering a competition option that included duct work for both front and rear drum brakes. Shown here is the small feeder duct (below three bright bolts) at the front wheel of a 1961 fuel-injected Corvette.

The C5 also hints at the legendary Corvette legacy with its "double-hump" dash, which mimics the first Sting Ray's dashboard. The passenger-side grab bar, shown here on a 1998 convertible, is also extremely reminiscent of the 1963–1967 Corvette.

Chevrolet introduced the C5 coupe first in 1997, then followed it up with a convertible in 1998. The convertible features the Corvette's first trunk since 1962. *Courtesy Chevrolet Motor Division, GM Corporation*

model-year intro. In May 1989, the project was moved back into 1994 as the engineering budget for the year was slashed. Three months later, the model year became 1995. It jumped again in October 1990 to 1996. By October 1992, the C5 was all but dead.

Corvette's second chief engineer, Dave McLellan, retired that fall, replaced by David Hill, who then saw the project through to its hard-fought finish. Retiring at the same time was the man who had tight-fistedly controlled the C5's early styling developments, Charles M. Jordan, GM's arrogant vice president of design who continually upset apple carts at the corporation by driving his Ferrari to work. His replacement, Wayne Cherry, was chosen over Jerry Palmer, head of Chevy 3 (the studio home to the Corvette since 1974) and the man responsible for the C4 restyle 10 years later. Palmer also oversaw John Cafaro, who rode the C5 project like a rodeo rider on a runaway bull—ups and downs and ins and outs often leaving him bothered and bewildered during the car's long and exhaustive, if not combative, design process.

General Manager Jim Perkins came into that fight in its earliest stages, returning to Chevrolet in January 1989 after spending five years launching Toyota's Lexus division. Unusually warm and down-to-earth for a man of his position, Perkins' role in the C5 play included some serious hocus-pocus with the books in early 1993 when things looked darkest for the developmental budget. He also in 1990 stood up against GM's highest offices, where some

FAR LEFT: GM Design exec Charles Jordan had the final say over early C5 styling work. He retired in 1992, by which time the 1997 Corvette's form was well established in Tech Center studios. *Copyright 1997 GM Corp. Used with permission GM Media Archives*

LEFT: Designer Jerry Palmer, the talented mind behind the C4 Corvette's look, oversaw the Design studios where the C5 Corvette took shape. *Copyright 1997 GM Corp. Used with permission GM Media Archives*

RIGHT: Jerry Palmer's main man in the Chevy 3 studio in Warren, Michigan, was John Cafaro. It was Cafaro's ideas that eventually prevailed during the C5 design process. *Courtesy Chevrolet Motor Division, GM Corporation*

FAR RIGHT: GM Interior Designer Jon Albert was in charge of making the C5 passenger compartment more comfortable and more user-friendly than ever before. *Courtesy Chevrolet Motor Division, GM Corporation*

Chevrolet has been lauded 11 times as *Motor Trend*'s Car (or Truck) of the Year. The C5 Corvette in 1998 made it four straight years that Chevy has taken home the coveted *Motor Trend* award. From left to right are Corvette Chief Engineer (and now Vehicle Line Executive) David Hill, Chevrolet General Manager John Middlebrook, Petersen Publishing President and Executive Publisher Lee Kelley, and Corvette Brand Manager Richard Almond.

felt the Corvette was an expensive frill the corporation could no longer afford, while still others hoped to take the car away from Chevrolet and make it a "General Motors Corvette." Perkins staved off both efforts. And it was his idea to build "Billy Bob," an entry-level Corvette priced in the $25,000–30,000 range. This car, the long-rumored "notchback coupe with a trunk," is scheduled to appear as a 1999 model just as this book is rolling off the presses in 1998. It will represent the first time the Corvette has ever been offered in three different model forms.

Although various differing executive opinions at GM surely contributed to the C5's rocky ride to market, the main impetus behind all the budget fights and rampant rescheduling was the corporation's financial crash to earth in 1992. In February 1989, GM officials had reported a profit of $4.86 billion for 1988, more than any other corporation in history. Two years later, however, that record gain had turned into a $2 billion record loss. But this paled weakly in comparison to the staggering $24.2 billion lost in 1992. Explaining this incredible turnaround is not simple;

The C5 shares next to no parts with its C4 forerunner; nearly all components were designed and manufactured exclusively for the all-new Corvette. *Courtesy Chevrolet Motor Division, GM Corporation*

major influences included new 1986 tax laws (that did away with car loan interest deductions) and equally new government safety regulations mandating air bags or passive restraints in all cars by 1990. By mid-1989, every automaker was feeling the bite created by these two federal actions as their cars became both more expensive to build and less affordable to the average Joe.

Adding insult to injury in GM's case was the way corporate leadership failed to face the future, then fell apart when it was needed the most. Having already lost the confidence of almost everyone below him, Chairman of the Board Roger Smith reached mandatory retirement in August 1990 at a time when hard decisions needed to be made to stem the tide of red ink. The financial nightmare facing new chairman Robert C. Stempel was almost overwhelming. Then Stempel, GM's former president, didn't help his position at all by naming Lloyd E. Reuss to fill the vacant president's seat, this against the opinions of various board members who questioned Reuss' management abilities. They were right. He failed miserably and was swept out the door with a demotion in 1992, replaced by Jack Smith, who was eventually responsible for finally giving the C5 project its official green light.

Like the nostalgic grab bar on the C5's dash, such soap operas themselves are nothing new in Corvette history. Roller-coaster rides and near-death experiences have come before, beginning with the first humble two-seater, which faced a premature end only a year after it was born. By the end of 1954 roughly a third of the 3,640 Corvettes built that year were still sitting unsold, and many decision makers at GM were wondering if it wasn't wise to cut and run. It was left to a new, powerful V-8 in 1955, coupled with the growing engineering emergence of Zora Duntov, to help turn things around.

An all-new, second-generation Corvette was also rumored for 1960, but it was three more years before the stunning Sting Ray debuted. Then, when the first Sting Ray's time came up, the revamped third-generation Corvette wasn't quite ready for the dance, leaving the so-called "midyear" model to roll on for one more year in 1967—to the eventual delight of collectors who generally agree that that last "unintended" second-generation Corvette ended up being the best of that short five-year run. A similar situation occurred when preparing the C4 for its planned debut. Stumbling blocks encountered during development and testing pushed that introduction back to March 1983, leading Chevrolet people to simply scrap the 1983 model-year designation, replacing it with a lengthened 1984 production run.

Intertwined throughout the Corvette's 45-year history is a long line of corporate skeptics who have, still do, and always will question the car's reason to live. At a mega-corporation now accustomed to building certain models by the hundreds of thousands and making money hand over fist, rolling out about 20,000 Corvettes a year that add "only" about $100 million annually to company coffers surely represents a paradox.

Compounding the issue is the way in which GM corporate mechanizations have progressed. Various reorganizations, performed over the years either in the best interests of modernizing and increasing efficiency or as part of Bob Stempel's efforts to right the ship in the early 1990s, have vastly changed the way Chevrolet and the other divisions build cars. Whereas the Corvette's fate used to be in the able hands of a few great movers and shakers—Harley Earl, Duntov, Bill Mitchell, etc.—the car today must be woven through a bureaucratic maze as big as Texas. In some minds, these modern complications not only helped prolong the C5 ordeal, they also may have compromised the results.

"GM's organization today is more efficient when it comes to bringing certain products to market," explained Paul Zazarine, group publisher vice president at *Corvette Fever* magazine, "but that doesn't mean, in the Corvette's case, that they did the job right this time. There is a certain degree of timidity in today's corporate world. No one wants to speak up; no one wants to stand out, and I think the new Corvette suffered for it."

Zazarine is impressed with all its new technologies and thrilling performance. "The C5 is exceptionally well

After about eight years of development work, the all-new C5 finally debuted in Detroit in January 1997. This 1997 coupe features the optional bodyside molding, a feature that even Corvette Brand Manager Richard Almond feels doesn't exactly do the car justice.

Chevrolet promotional people were exceptionally proud of the new C5 convertible's trunk, which they said can hold, not one, but two bags of golf clubs. This claim far and away has been recited in the press more than any other involving the C5's merits. Is the best 'Vette yet also the best golf cart yet? *Courtesy Chevrolet Motor Division, GM Corporation*

done; the wind-tunnel-tested body, the aluminum LS1, the brakes, the frame, the ergonomics—everything nuts and bolts about the car is terrific." Yet the former *Corvette Fever* editor still feels something doesn't quite add up. "You hear people today talk about cars using the 'sum of the parts' proposition," he said. "Totaled up, everything that goes into the car added together is greater than those parts, those features, on their own. The new Corvette is somehow different. If you look at each individual part, each area is so well done, so exceptional. But this is one time where the sum of the parts is less." Defying physical laws? Maybe. That aside, Zazarine does believe the C5 has fallen short of expectations.

"The car should have been more dynamic," he said. "When the 1968 Corvette hit the road, there was nothing else like it. The '84 was a handsome car; again there was nothing else like it out there." Zazarine does agree that Chevrolet did manage to preserve at least some of the grand Corvette vestiges but not to the degree that all the typical press-release hyperbole has claimed. "Put an '84 next to an earlier Corvette, and you see the heritage. Put a '97 next to a '96, and I really don't see the same thing." Additionally, he

feels the C5 has been adorned with too many vestiges of other cars, both inside and out of GM. "When I get into a C5, I feel like I'm driving a Trans Am or a Z28." In his opinion, the styling process must have gone like this: "take a meat grinder, pour in Porsche Boxster, NSX, Trans Am, 3000GT, RX-7, turn the crank, and out came the '97 Corvette."

Zazarine's not alone in his feelings. According to *Sports Car International* editor D. Randy Riggs, brand character took up too big a part in the mix. "There's way too much F-body in there," he said. "It looks like a Camaro that has been squashed by Godzilla." Wes Raynal, editor at *Corvette Quarterly*, was nowhere near as harsh. "When I saw the first pictures, I wasn't too psyched," he began. "When I saw it at the [Detroit] Auto Show, I thought 'ho-hum.' But when I saw it on the road, I liked it a lot better."

"Design, look, style, whatever you call it, it is always in the eye of the beholder," responded Corvette Brand Manager Richard Almond to critics' claims that the new Corvette doesn't look as sensational as it should. "I think this is the most attractive thing in the world," he said. "It is a great looking car." Nonetheless, Almond does agree about the resemblances to other sports cars. "There is a similarity to the [Acura] NSX, and rightly so. The dynamics of physics determine that to get that low coefficient of drag, you're going to end up with similar bodies."

As he explained further, wind-tunnel testing also produced the target of most critics, the car's tail, which Riggs says "is too big and bulbous." "The entire car is physically huge for a two-passenger automobile," he added. Still others have complained about the tail's abrupt nature, its sharp edges. "I do understand the individual design factors behind that new look," said Almond. "That clipped rear end has a reason to be, due to aerodynamic testing."

Kurt Romberg, the aerodynamic engineer responsible for that look, put it this way, "You look at the rear of the car, you're going to see a hard edge across the deck and a hard edge that runs down the side of the quarters. That is there specifically for aerodynamics. We spent a lot of time locating that hard edge, and what it does is it separates the air cleanly off the car."

Even considering how tightly form does follow function in the C5's case, Paul Zazarine still feels the car has stumbled from a gut feeling perspective. What does he credit for this result? "The Corvette no longer is the product of the passions of one specific mind," he continued. "The C5 needed to be uniquely Corvette; the '68 was; the '84 was. The '68 Corvette came from Bill Mitchell; the '84 Corvette came from Jerry Palmer. The C5 was done by committee. It's a terrific car, but it lacks soul. Somewhere down the line [it has] lost the spirit." He, of course, blames changing times and changing ways. "The '68 Corvette could not have been done under the current GM regime," he concluded.

Soul. Spirit. Charm. Persona. Of course such things are so typically subjective. And even Zazarine admits his stance might paint him up in some minds as a purist, a dirty word nowadays when so many seem so eager to jump on the latest high-tech bandwagon and ride it into what their blind faith tells them must be a better future.

At least the Corvette still has a future, and what appears right now as a reasonably bright one at that.

Ray Quinlan thinks so, and he qualifies as a purist right up with the staunchest of them. Seventy-seven-year-old Quinlan has been a fiberglass fanatic since he saw his first Corvette in 1953 at GM's Motorama in Chicago. He has owned them since 1958. And today, he holds lifetime membership number one from the National Corvette Museum Foundation, this in honor of him donating his 1953 Corvette to the NCM group many years before there ever was a museum building to display it in. Even in his advanced years, this forever-young car buff can still be seen making the 1,000-mile trek from his home in Champaign, Illinois, to Winter Haven, Florida, for the annual Cypress Gardens Corvette Show. In his 1963 Sting Ray roadster. With the top down.

In Quinlan's minds, the older solid-axle cars of pre-1963 were the best Corvettes ever. Were. As much as he loves his 1953 and 1957, he can't say enough about the C5. "I think it is the greatest car ever made; mechanically, aerodynamically, functionally, practically—from a price perspective—there's nothing else in the world like it." And styling? "I love it. It ties back to the past and looks ahead to the future."

How far ahead, as always, is up to a group of forever-old GM execs.

Regardless of whether or not you think a hundred-mill is a paltry profit, Corvettes have always paid their way. And the car's value as both a sexy market tease and rolling testbed for other Chevrolet products cannot be denied, no matter how much corporate sticks-in-the-mud try. "This car is important to GM," explained John Middlebrook, "and based on the attention it's getting from the press and the sports car buying public, it's an important car to America's culture."

Too bad not all GM minds think like Middlebrook. America's sports car commonly has been rumored to be that close (hold up your thumb and forefinger in proximity) to extinction. Thankfully, from a Corvette lover's perspective, the triumphant C5 has put those thoughts to rest, at least for a few more years.

It would be easy enough to point at the C5 tale and laugh; after all, could an automaker possibly complicate a development process any more than General Motors did when it came time to build a next-generation Corvette? Ah, but therein awaits the rub. Considering just how great the Corvette has been for more than four decades now, isn't it only right to expect that the greatest American sports car would require more sweat, more thought, even more conflict than ever before?

Besides, any other mere mortal of an automobile would have never survived such an ordeal, nor would it have been given the chance. The C5's ride to production was long and hard because the car itself was so deserving of such a Herculean effort, such an epic fight. Homer just might have written about this four-wheeled odyssey, and then the Corvette truly would have been preserved for the ages.

For now, perhaps Middlebrook's prose will do. "Corvette is much more than just a car," he said. "It's a love affair. Words alone fail to convey the passion it inspires."

Enough said.

CHAPTER ONE

BEGGARS CAN BE CHOOSY
Designing the C5

Two-hundred-fifty-million bucks. That's all they wanted. To build a totally redesigned Y-car, an all-new Corvette. Hell, when Chrysler redid its mini-van in 1996, the company reportedly spent $675.8 million, just on tools and dies. Chrysler's research and development bill on its own came to $247 million. Chevrolet wanted to build an entire car, a far more advanced vehicle at that, for not much more than that latter figure. It all looked so laughable, especially so after Ford reportedly spent $2.8 *billion* in the early 1990s on its revamped Taurus. Revamped, not redesigned.

Yet as much as the C5 program looked like the bargain of the century, collecting that needed cash was in no way easy for Jim Perkins, David Hill, John Cafaro, and the rest. One moment it was there. Then it wasn't. Then some

of it was. GM's world-class financial woes, which began seeping into this story just as the 1980s wound down, were, of course, to blame for the long line of budget cuts and review board meetings. But so too was more than one decision maker who just couldn't find a place in the corporation's ever-reorganizing scheme of things for such a narrow-focused product like Corvette, a car obviously limited in the way it generates corporate revenue.

Not that the Corvette hasn't carried its own weight; it has. What concerned many GM upper-crusters was how well an all-new rendition could continue doing so, especially considering the lofty goals set down for the C5 from the beginning. This was not only meant to be the fastest, best-performing Corvette ever, it was also going to be the most functional, most practical, most comfortable, most

Rival automakers should be upset. What Chevrolet did with "only" $250 million borders on unbelievable. That's how much it cost to build an entirely new Corvette for 1997.

This Jerry Palmer rendering, dated August 1989, demonstrates that a basic underlying theme was present throughout the design process. Remember also that the C5 Corvette was designed first as a convertible. *Copyright 1996 GM Corp. Used with permission GM Media Archives*

This later rendering, done by Dan Magda, John Cafaro's deputy studio chief at Chevy 3, shows off the same geometric shape that carried through to the end. Notice the radically different diameter wheels, an idea Cafaro was especially fond of. *Copyright 1996 GM Corp. Used with permission GM Media Archives*

convenient. All this and it wasn't going to gain anything in price. Or weight. It was going to bring home the bacon too. On that, Hill and the gang felt they couldn't lose. GM execs weren't so sure.

Can you blame them? Here was a plan featuring so many unproven parts. An all-aluminum pushrod V-8 that was at the same time lighter yet sturdier and able to pump out upwards of 350 horsepower. An incredibly rigid backbone frame with a tunnel center-section and immensely strong side rails formed by water pressure, a new process that had yet to be applied on such a scale. A rear-mounted transmission that gave the car better balance and more interior room. An out-of-this-world body that was both stunning to look at and slippery in the wind tunnel to the tune of a 0.29 drag coefficient, an unprecedented automotive aerodynamic achievement.

This project represented a clean sheet of paper unlike any other previously turned page in GM history. So much so, not even the men who were writing the C5 story themselves could agree on the word choice.

Budget battles were one thing; ego clashes were another. Carlisle "Cardy" Davis, Corvette program manager, didn't approve of Chief Engineer Dave McLellan's management style. McLellan and Design Vice President Chuck Jordan liked a mid-engined layout. But Chevrolet General Manager Jim Perkins was hot for the front engine, rear transmission idea. Chevy 3 studio head John Cafaro didn't like the way Jordan ran the Design ship; then again, almost no one else working under the "Chrome Cobra" did either—even more so after he secretly arranged a three-way C5 design competition between Cafaro's group, Tom Peters' Advanced 4 studio in Detroit, and John Schinella's Advanced Concepts Center (ACC) in California. Finally, everyone, Design and Engineering alike, had no use for short-time GM president Lloyd Reuss.

Time healed some of these early wounds. Jordan would finally retire in late 1992, replaced by Wayne Cherry and Jerry Palmer in a diplomatic tag-team arrangement. Although Cherry was actually chosen over Palmer as Jordan's replacement atop Design in September that year, the move was more of a title shuffle than a displacement. Cherry's job description involved more business than art; he would handle the budget and overall operation of GM Design. Palmer was made director of Design for the newly formed North American Operations group. He would still run the studios and influence actual designs.

Campaigning for his mid-engined idea right up to the end, McLellan eventually grew weary of the whole affair and took early retirement in August 1992, ending his 17-year reign as Zora Duntov's replacement. Filling McLellan's big shoes in November 1992 was former Cadillac engineer David Hill.

Early in 1992, Joe Spielman, Cardy Davis' new boss, decided he needed Cardy's talents in an even more challenging program and reassigned him to the floundering W-car (Chevy Lumina, Pontiac Grand Prix, etc.) team. In Davis' place came Russ McLean. Spielman himself then was reassigned in October 1994, with Cadillac/Luxury Car Division General Manager Don Hackworth taking over the top Midsize Car Division position as part of an eventual merger between CLCD and MCD. During his two-year stay atop MCD, Spielman had transformed a $1.5 billion deficit into $150 million worth of black ink.

Even Cafaro found himself eventually moving on to another challenge late in 1994 as Jim Perkins asked him to

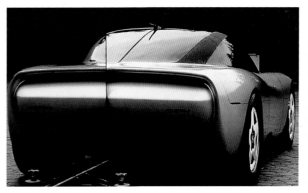

head up the design process of yet another future Chevy product. Part of Cafaro's new deal was that he would continue controlling what the C5 looks like until 1999.

Up at the business end, GM Chairman of the Board Roger Smith retired in August 1990, leaving the whole mess to Bob Stempel, who then picked Reuss as president. Reuss was forced out of office in the spring of 1992, replaced by Jack Smith. And after receiving a no-confidence vote from the board on October 22, 1992, Stempel himself stepped down. John Smale then stepped in. At Chevrolet Jim Perkins took over as general manager in January 1989 after Bob Burger retired.

Additional corporate structure changes came courtesy of various reorganizations along the way as first Stempel, then Smale, attempted to turn General Motors around. Three such Stempel reorganizations alone came in the desperate—for both GM and its not-long-for-this-world chairman—year of 1992, the worst financial time in corporation history and one of the darkest moments for the C5 project. Everything basically came to a head in October that year. After an October 19 meeting where McLean told a dozen or so top C5 people that Stempel had put yet another hold on the new Corvette, Pete Liccardello, a model-year manager, could manage only one word to describe the project's status: "chaos."

An earlier Stempel-inspired reorganization in mid-1991 eventually led to the dissolution of the Chevrolet-

This rough clay depicts a rear-end approach very reminiscent of the F-body style. Commonly heard complaints concerning C5 styling involve how much the new Corvette looks like its Camaro cousin. *Courtesy Chevrolet Motor Division, GM Corporation*

Pontiac-Canada group, the Corvette's home, in 1992. This particular restructuring resulted in the Y-car losing much of its independence, its autonomy, while the corporate maze was growing ever more tangled with procedures and pecking orders.

By 1996 additional restructuring had taken the division general managers out of the loop. They no longer had any say about future cars; these chores were now handled by a newly created collection of vehicle line engineers and brand managers. Dick Almond was the new brand manager for Corvette and F-body (Camaro and Firebird). David Hill was given the Corvette VLE position in October 1995. After playing a major role running interference for the C5, Jim Perkins found himself all but out of the picture in 1996. He then took early retirement.

This rendering shows much of the final C5 form—the "double-bubble" roof, the hood's subtle contours, the bodyside scallops. Wind-tunnel demands, as well as subjective opinions, probably ruled out this attractive nose, which does appear much more distinctive than the final result. Nose treatments represented one of the more hotly debated aspects of the C5 design. *Copyright 1996 GM Corp. Used with permission GM Media Archives*

The "October revolution" of 1992 had not only let the world know GM was floundering, it also produced another new organization, the Vehicle Launch Center (VLC), a place were new-car programs would roll through on the way to earning big-money approval, a process itself already complicated enough. GM had initiated its latest such process in the 1980s, calling it "Four-Phase," even though it actually had five phases. And the final one was labeled "Phase Three." Go figure.

The first of the five phases was called "bubble-up." Creative juices, get it? Here, Design and Engineering teams began letting the ideas flow with the goal being to reach Concept Initiation (CI), which was a formal review of those ideas by GM execs. Once past CI, the project would move into Phase Zero, where specifications were finalized, a budget established, and a business plan put into place. Design's work would be done. In Phase One, parts would be ordered and early test cars built and run. Assembly plant conversion plans would also be made. Final testing came in Phase Two, as did official production. Phase Three involved "continuous production and improvement." Along the way a new car would roll through various reviews, or "gates." The whole deal would supposedly require 48 months. When the VLC emerged, it was intended to effectively "marry" bubble-up and Phase Zero.

Want more structure? In January 1993, Mike Juras joined MCD as its engineering director under Joe Spielman. In April, Juras instituted his own reorganization, his "Juras Vision," a plan that stripped the Y-car of even more autonomy, unduly complicated development further, and left almost everyone on the C5 project wondering how the hell it all worked. When Juras was given early retirement in March 1995, they all finally stopped wondering and went back to work.

Weaving its way through the corporate approval process was a long, convoluted trip for the C5. Its first Concept Initiation was scheduled for March 23, 1989. As mentioned, initial budget estimates came in at $250 million, more than enough money to build a truly historic

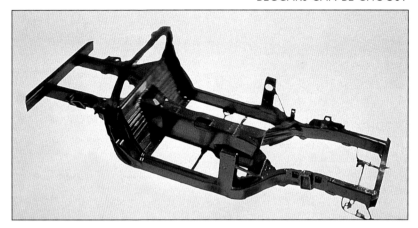

Key to so many of the C5 Corvette's newfound solid attributes is its welded-up frame. This exceptionally rugged foundation features a strong central-tunnel section and ultra-precise, super-stiff, one-piece tubular side rails formed by water pressure. *Courtesy Chevrolet Motor Division, GM Corporation*

Corvette, thought Jerry Palmer. Then Cardy Davis was given only $210 million. The car could be done for $210 million but not the interior he told Chevrolet-Pontiac-Canada (CPC) head Mike Mutchler.

Lloyd Reuss oversaw the CI, which brought together Davis, Mutchler, Palmer, and McLellan. Mutchler's opinion was that that extra $40 million for the interior could wait a couple years. Considering that the goal was the best 'Vette yet, most agreed that a new car with an old interior wouldn't do. Reuss okayed the $250 million. Things were good. For the moment.

Eight days later, Reuss announced he had concerns, which would be addressed in another meeting six weeks later. In April, Mutchler informed Davis not to worry about that meeting. Money was getting tight at GM and budget cuts had already pushed the C5 back from a 1993 model to a 1994. That was just the beginning.

Originally built by John Schinella's Advanced Concepts Center in California in the summer of 1990, the sexy Sting Ray III concept car was a big hit at Detroit's North American International Auto Show in January 1992. Many hoped it would end up being the next-generation Corvette. Here, the Sting Ray III wings its way around the GM Tech Center test track in March 1992. *Tom Glatch*

By July 1989, Roger Smith and Stempel knew even more cutbacks lay ahead. At CPC, the losses for 1989 would reach $1 billion, $1.3 billion for 1990, leading Mutchler to consider funneling even more money away from C5 to help shore up other programs. Later in October, Stempel stood up before his top 1,000 executives at GM's annual executive conference in Traverse City, Michigan, and began reciting a long list of additional cutbacks. On this list was the C5, which from then was put on "indefinite status." At best, the new Corvette was now a 1995 model. If that.

To keep things progressing without an official budget, C5 work was creatively charged to the C4 project. More book-juggling came later. Right after Christmas 1992, Jim Perkins agreed to let the C5 project have $1 million of Chevrolet money, this to build a running test mule, the Corvette Engineering Research Vehicle number four. Unlike its three mid-engined forefathers (CERV I was built in 1960, CERV II in 1962, CERV III in 1989), CERV IV wasn't meant to be a show car. Its goal was to test as many C5 features as possible while still looking much like a 1993 Corvette—except for its trunk.

TDM, Inc., in Livonia, Michigan, needed only 91 days and $1.2 million to complete the CERV IV with its bastardized C4 body, backbone chassis, rear transaxle, ZR-1 tail, and standard small-block V-8. The last-mentioned was used because the Gen III V-8 (for more on this, see chapter 3) was then in its early stages of development. Hill's testing crew would have to make do with a mere mortal engine until a testable Gen III could be made ready.

After this car was completed in May 1993, it was determined a second one could be built for only about $600,000. Thus, a CERV IVb was then planned to join the renamed CERV IVa. It was delivered in January 1994 with an iron-block Gen III V-8 as the planned aluminum cylinder block had yet to pass muster.

These two CERV vehicles would carry the testing load until Chevrolet could officially build its "alpha" and "beta" test cars. Both the alpha and beta were rough-and-

One of the more popular improvements offered by the C5 design is the lower door-sill height, this made possible by those super-strong perimeter frame rails. Notice the difference as a driver exits a 1994 C4 convertible (left) and the new 1998 droptop.

ready test machines, although a beta would show a little more completion and refinement than the alpha. Pete Liccardello in April 1993 announced a schedule for these preproduction testbeds. According to Hill, about 10 to 20 alphas would be built with C5 bodies, not as modified C4s like the CERV IVa. Correcting alpha mistakes would result in the beta build. Then would come real prototypes, followed by pre-pilot cars and pilot cars, the latter actually available for sale. Pre-pilots would come off the Bowling Green line in August 1996, pilots in September.

For then, early in 1993, all the test team had was the CERV IVa. Building it and billing it directly to Chevrolet were both done in complete secrecy. Spielman, Perkins, and the few others who knew of the project all figured it was just best to get a test car rolling and worry about

facing bean counters' music later. That came in June 1993 when auditors discovered the "missing million" and began looking for a suspected embezzler. Perkins confessed and offered to resign or repay the money himself. By then the CERV IV was already running on test tracks. GM paper-pushers just shrugged their shoulders and walked away.

Back in the spring of 1990, the C5 group had realized all they needed was an additional $2 million for the engineering budget to begin real work in August 1990, which translated into the proper starting point for a 48-month Four-Phase process, resulting in production of an all-new 1995 Corvette. Mutchler turned them down in April, leaving the car again in limbo.

In October, Reuss pushed the C5 back yet again to 1996. If GM didn't start making money, he said, that model year might move back even further. Come spring 1991, the proposed C5 budget had dropped to $150 million, and some witnesses even heard talk of closing down the Bowling Green plant. Another CI was finally planned for August. Then September. Then October. Then never.

In March 1992, Spielman announced another fall back, this one to 1997. He also mentioned that the CI would be rescheduled for January 1993. In between, GM's October 1992 crisis meetings validated the latest model-year delay, the fourth in three years. Then, come January 1993, the CI was again moved back, this time to June. A second C5 "gate," Concept Alternatives Selection (CAS)—the process where every major component option is reviewed—was then set up for August 10. Normally, the GM plan would leave four or five months between CI and CAS; the C5 team was given only 57 days to get ready.

As 1993 dawned, David Hill made note of two main priorities for the C5 project: less vehicle weight and more money, much more than the $150 million then being discussed. It was also soon realized that the existing C4 Corvette would never meet the new federally mandated side-impact standards for 1997, and to bring it up to spec would cost $80 million. A decision on the C5 needed to be made soon or Chevrolet risked missing the 1997 model

With a spare tire deleted from the design, the C5 was able to offer more rear cargo space than any previous Corvette. Also making this possible was a clever dual gas tank arrangement that tucked nicely behind each seat—they can be seen straddling the transmission in the bottom illustration. Notice the connecting lines between the tanks. *Courtesy Chevrolet Motor Division, GM Corporation*

Another major C5 innovation is its rear-mounted transmission, which is tied to the aluminum LS1 V-8 by a torque tube running through the frame's central tunnel. Also notice the transverse-mounted, reverse-flow mufflers with twin tailpipes at the rear of the upper illustration. *Courtesy Chevrolet Motor Division, GM Corporation*

Shown here with Cafaro's "Black Car" are various people who made it possible. From left to right are: Randy Wittine, Steve Allen, Steve Resin, Dave Snabes, Dan Robar, Clay Dean, Jim Adair, Gary Clark, Claudia Bertolin, Dave Cubitt, and Ron Nowicki. *Copyright 1996 GM Corp. Used with permission GM Media Archives*

John Cafaro's "Black Car" was probably the second most popular C5 styling study behind the Sting Ray III show car built by the Advanced Concepts Center in California. *Copyright 1996 GM Corp. Used with permission GM Media Archives*

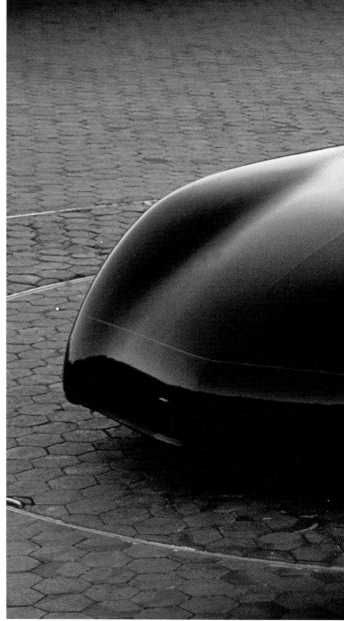

year entirely, much like the C4 had done in 1983. Spielman then pledged to get the budget back up to $250 million—they couldn't miss that 1997 deadline.

In March, Russ McLean began preparations for the upcoming CI before GM president Jack Smith. His latest budget plan called for $241 million.

Everything seemed on track until the end of the month when Hill made the mistake of talking with *Automotive News* Engineering Editor Jack Keebler. Hill dodged most questions but let slip a comment concerning the Corvette's need to turn a profit. Keebler took it from there.

"Corvette Must Tally a Profit or It Dies," screamed the *Automotive News* cover story for March 29. "David Hill is

locked in a life-or-death struggle to keep the Corvette alive," wrote Keebler. "And the odds are stacked against him." Although Hill did talk about the stumbling blocks awaiting a next-generation design, he by no means meant for Keebler to think Chevrolet was anywhere near giving up on the Corvette. He was shocked. All those hard at work on the C5 were shocked. Corvette owners, past, present, and future, were shocked. It was a few months before GM officials were able to convince the last skeptic that the end was not near.

When the C5 team finally did come before Smith on June 14, 1993, it was explained that for that $241 million, GM would sell 25,000 C5s a year over a seven-year life span. The team had been in bubble-up for five years now, said Spielman; they must surely have this thing down. Smith agreed and gave his approval, influenced at least partly by the shiny, black CERV IVa displayed before him.

But the battle wasn't over yet. Another gate, Concept Direction (CD), came along in October 1993, after which time the C5 plan would be locked in. After CD would come the final Concept Approval (CA), with Smith again presiding. Real cars with real Gen III engines would be running on tracks after CA.

In early May 1994, the C5 team again went before Smith's review board. This time, they showed off a bright red C5 Corvette replica, a model that cost Chevrolet a half a million to build. That review resulted in heavy questioning from Executive Vice President J. T. Battenberg, who also happened to be head of GM's Components Group. Battenberg claimed the C5 team had reached the final approval stage without tying down all parts suppliers; this a definite no-no. He was right. Hill's response was that they had had barely 10 months in Phase Zero, while McLean explained that a final purchasing plan was working and all supplier contracts would be signed within two months.

But Battenberg wouldn't quit. Additional points of contention involved how the Bowling Green plant would trade C4 production for C5. In the end, Spielman defended the team by pointing out what a great job they had managed under such severe circumstances. Convinced,

These 1/8-scale models were used to demonstrate what a difference a year can make. At left is 1996; at right is what 1997 might have looked like. *Copyright 1995 GM Corporation Used with permission GM Media Archives*

Smith gave conditional approval, with a stipulation that the team report back in June carrying a plan to convert the C4 line into the C5.

Immediately afterward, Ron Haas, vice president for quality, faxed Mutchler and Spielman questioning many untried engineering practices and the fact that no "design intent" vehicles had been built yet. He described C5 as an extremely high-risk program. When they dismissed his contentions, Haas faxed them to Smith, who then instructed the C5 team to come clean with a demonstration vehicle.

At June's meeting back in front of Smith's Strategy Board, McLean answered Haas' claim with the CERV IVa, which had been undergoing testing for almost a year by then. McLean considered it to be a demonstration vehicle, the first alpha car. Haas didn't agree, claiming it didn't really demonstrate fully the advanced aspects of the C5. Mutchler jumped in saying he couldn't increase the engineering budget to build experimental cars. They weren't cheap. Alphas and betas cost about $750,000 each. McLean pointed out how much testing they were

Yes, it looks like the real thing. But what appears to be a bright red C5 coupe is in fact a foil-covered clay model. The 1996 Corvette behind it on the Tech Center Patio in Warren, Michigan, is real. *Copyright 1996 GM Corp. Used with permission GM Media Archives*

Typically brutalized and heavily disguised to fool spy photographers, this rough-looking character is a C5 alpha car, a very early prototype that went into production in June 1994. The crude, flat-black alphas were later joined by the more developed beta models, which were painted white. *Courtesy Chevrolet Motor Division, GM Corporation*

getting for the dollar at that point. And he also laid out the numbers for merging C5 into assembly line traffic—it was this expense that helped bring the final budget number to $250 million. Smith agreed with it all. The C5 was no longer "provisional." Concept Approval was finally given. With no strings. The deal was done.

And to think the project had begun almost six years before with the first sketches made in a secret room in the basement of the GM Technical Center in Warren, Michigan. Upstairs was John Cafaro's Chevy 3 studio, long home to the Corvette's future. Chuck Jordan had ordered Cafaro to set up shop in that basement room in August 1988 with the intention being to open a "Corvette Skunk Works," a refuge where the next-generation Y-car could be born in complete privacy. There, the clays were first sculpted of what both Cafaro and Jordan then thought would be the all-new 1993 Corvette. Silly them.

Styling the C5 was almost as tough as passing Concept Approval. Jordan saw to that. He disapproved of almost everything put before him early on and seemingly took pleasure in turning drawing tables over whenever he could—figuratively, of course. Then again, just maybe he wanted to see his people do the best job they could to produce the best Corvette ever seen. He certainly had all the best people for the job.

John Cafaro thought he was the best man in the spring of 1989. At that time, his Chevy 3 studio was busy completing the new Camaro, then planned for 1992. Once the Camaro was done, Cafaro's men could give the Y-car their full attention. But a week before Chevy 3 was to release the F-body design in January, Chuck Jordan ordered a laundry list of changes, these inspired by a wild Camaro show car built earlier by John Schinella's Advanced Concepts Center (ACC) in Newbury Park, a northwest suburb of Los Angeles.

Jordan hated Chevy 3's proposals anyway, and he told Cafaro if he couldn't do better, Schinella's West Coast boys could. Then he immediately ordered Schinella to go ahead with a "California Corvette." Jordan also ordered Tom Peters in the Advanced 4 studio to make it a three-way contest, all this without telling Cafaro anything. Cafaro's opinion of Jordan only worsened once he found out.

Two weeks before the C5's first CI in March 1989, Jordan ordered Cafaro to show his team's work for approval; two renditions were picked and transformed into full-size clays. But later that summer, in a fit of pique, Jordan temporarily took Cafaro off the project and put Peters into the driver's seat. He also demanded that Schinella's group not only produce a clay but an actual running car, this to come by summer 1990. Back East, Cafaro and Peters both knew that the California Corvette, like its earlier Camaro concept counterpart, would be a wild one, yet not practical at all.

Cafaro soon eased his way back into the design race, just in time to see ACC's results. Schinella's California Corvette appeared in the spring of 1990. It was purple and sleek and sexy and topless. It was the Sting Ray III, and it also had a trunk, something Corvettes had gone without since 1962. Once in Detroit, the Sting Ray III was not all that well-liked by the C5 teamers there. But it did end up being the hit at the Detroit International Auto Show in January 1992.

With the gauntlet thrown down by the Sting Ray III, it was left to the guys back in Detroit to make Jordan happy. That became easier as the shape evolved, each time growing closer to the timeless ideal the GM Design chief had in mind. In April 1991, another show was put on displaying competing C5 designs. Jordan picked a model by Peters but qualified his choice by also directing the designers to add much of Cafaro's proposal into it. In late March 1992, Cafaro showed off his "Black Car" along with the Sting Ray III and others in another Design show. The Black Car was based on the C4's birdcage chassis, but it looked hot and could be remounted onto the backbone frame then being developed by Engineering. Jim Perkins liked the look, which did predict quite a bit of the final product.

From there that look was scraped, hammered, beaten, and blown into shape, all this coming with more than a little help from John Q. Public. Like all automakers today,

Deleting a spare tire was made possible by the inclusion of Goodyear's Extended Mobility tires, or "run-flats," as standard equipment. This National Corvette Museum display depicts Goodyear's first EMT design, offered as a C4 Corvette option beginning in 1994. The C5's run-flat tires are of a revised style.

Chevrolet has for some time now actually been interested in what its customers have to say about its products. A valuable component of the design process now is the customer clinic, where artwork, models, and even mockups are shown to a group of consumers picked from either the division's own buyer base or a competitor's. Or both. Their opinions then are factored into future work.

For C5, an important clinic was held in November 1992. Almost 300 people looked at photos of four different proposals. One thing they liked was the "double-bubble" roof. A similar idea was demonstrated atop the taillights of one car. Jerry Palmer didn't like this effect. Neither did consumers at the clinic. Any wonder why it later disappeared?

A second clinic came in June 1993 in Los Angeles. Four murals of different proposals were again displayed; one showing the work of Cafaro and Dan Magda, a second from Randy Wittine of Chevy 3, the third from Joe Ponce of Advanced 2, and the last from ACC. The last wasn't received well at all. The other three were reasonably liked with most of the participants pointing out that they'd prefer to mix this aspect here with that one over there. Negatives weren't nearly as bad as those of the November clinic, so Cafaro and crew basically felt they'd won the day. From there up into October, the C5 form really started shaping up as refinements began taking hold.

Of course, much of how this shape went together had to do with what would be hidden beneath it. While Design and Engineering often end up like oil and water, they do, periodically, have to work together to make sure form ends up working in concert with function. This relationship is even more important in the Corvette's case, much more so in the case of the C5 Corvette, the best functioning fiberglass form ever.

Two major functions influenced the C5's design equation: aerodynamics and chassis geometry. Hill's goal for the former was a drag coefficient (Cd) of 0.29, better than anything else on the road. Bar none. By the summer of 1993, wind-tunnel tests had shown the C5 only able to hit a 0.319 Cd—very good, but still not worthy of best-yet status. It wasn't long before the clay scrapers had done all they could on the top to cheat the wind. It was then left to aerodynamics engineer Kurt Romberg to add three belly pans underneath the car to "clean up" that side, too. Remember, air also flows below the body. When it was all said and done, the C5 did reach that 0.29 score—the lowest, by far, for any American production car.

Choosing a chassis was another tough job. By October 1989, the engineering team was showing ideas for two unique concepts, an all-wheel-drive (AWD) Corvette and a totally new "backbone" frame to replace the birdcage chassis used by the C4. This design featured a strong central "tunnel" and massive, one-piece side rails tied together by cross-members. Unlike the C4's birdcage, which allowed the car to flex too much, this backbone frame would make the C5 as solid as a rock, even in convertible form. It would also be lighter and allow the car to sit lower.

Yet another benefit was the low door-sill height allowed by those reshaped rails. Previous Corvette's had to draw their strength from their huge side rails, which forced drivers to climb in over them. This new frame didn't need all that bulk beneath each door, thus the sill could be closer to the ground and easier to step over.

It was a great idea on paper. Manufacturing it was another story. To produce the strength and precise specifications required for these 15-foot-long, one-piece, steel tubes bent in various vectors meant an innovative process was needed.

That process is called hydroforming, a new practice using extreme water pressure to literally "blow up" steel tubes into desired shapes. Hydroforming the C5's frame rails requires some truly huge dies into which the pre-bent, welded, steel tubes are rested. Once the tube is trapped between a mating die, water is pumped into the sealed-off tube at 6,000 pounds per square inch. This molecule-mashing fluid pressure then reshapes the round tube into a rectangular rail.

Presto, instant one-piece frame rail in exacting specs—no two are unlike. Translated, they're all identical. Since C4 frames required many welding operations, tiny differences always resulted section to section, frame to frame, meaning you couldn't quite count on suspension precision since overall stiffness, general consistency, and precise physical geometry couldn't be guaranteed. As exacting as it possibly gets, the hydroformed rails helped make the backbone frame the only choice as the C5's foundation.

By late 1989, Advance Vehicle Engineering counted 47 C5 project items already funded and being worked on. Among the top four listed was the backbone frame.

Jerry Palmer, however, didn't like the backbone for various reasons. One involved the way it clashed with his hopes for a mid-engined Corvette, a design that Jordan and McLellan also supported. When GM closed for Christmas 1989, Palmer had five scale-model Corvettes in the Advanced 4 studio. Two were mid-engined.

On February 28, 1990, Jordan scheduled yet another show of ideas, this time for Cardy Davis, Mike Mutchler, and Perkins. At this meeting, Mutchler told Palmer the mid-engined idea would never fly. But another idea was then gaining ground, this one keeping the engine in front while moving the transmission to the back. Not only would this layout allow more interior space, it would also—like the mid-engined arrangement—bring the car's balance closer to a 50/50 weight bias. It might open up more space for all-wheel-drive, too.

One of Tom Peters' proposals was an AWD, rear transaxle car that impressed Mutchler and Perkins. Perkins also liked Palmer's front engine/rear transaxle models. McLellan disliked the rear transaxle package; he, of course, still wanted a mid-engined Corvette. At this time, Perkins also brought up his idea for an entry-level, two-wheel-drive car, an affordable model aimed at younger buyers. This was his "Billy Bob" Corvette.

The convertible-with-a-trunk idea, demonstrated excitedly by the Sting Ray III, began drawing more and more attention by the summer of 1990. In the spring of 1991, the C5 team formalized the proposed three-car line-up: targa hardtop, convertible, and fixed-roof "Billy Bob" coupe. That last car had a trunk just like the convertible. Lloyd Reuss liked this proposal, which would've been part of the team's Concept Initiation presentation originally scheduled for August 1991. Would've been. That CI, of course, never came.

Nor did the mid-engined Corvette. A meeting early in 1992, following months of design risk analysis, finally put McLellan's pet design to rest. And in turn gave a thumbs-up to the front engine/rear transmission plan. Design evolution also produced a longer wheelbase and wider track for the C5, these expansions made for more than one reason.

Putting the wheels farther apart in both dimensions increased stability. It also opened up more design lee-way involving passenger compartment room and engine location. The Gen III V-8, without a transmission trailing it, could be moved farther back since the passenger compartment itself was set back and its size was no longer controlled by the transmission's intrusion. Stability again benefited since the new engine location, like the rear-mounted transmission/transaxle, helped move the C5's weight balance rearward. This balance is what Zora Duntov had wanted all along.

David Hill's decision to roll the targa-top C5 out first for 1997, followed by the convertible in 1998, then the coupe, came in the summer of 1993. Even though Engineering had from the outset designed the frame to be stiff enough to support a convertible without any extra bracing, Design had made the targa-top its main priority and had yet to do much work on the droptop model by August 1993. Thus an open Corvette was left to wait a year. As you're reading this, the coupe is lurking about somewhere as a 1999 model.

Not so much a matter of convenience as it was a response to subjective complaints was the choice of analog instruments instead of the "computer-game" digital dashes incorporated in the C4. Magazine reviewers had never tired of poking fun at the C4 dash, so C5 designers took away the butt of their jokes.

The list of additional decisions, of give and take between Design and Engineering, is of course long, dealing with everything from interior knobs to fitting the Gen III V-8 beneath the hood. That latter task was not easy as a low nose was both important to wind-tunnel testing and the view from behind the wheel. A C4 driver can barely see over the hood compared to his C5 counterpart. This design priority was just one of many driver-friendly functions dialed into the design.

Hill told Cafaro he would fit an engine beneath that low, sloping hood at any cost, and that he did. The Gen III's extreme rearward location helped a lot, as did a unique, almost flat oil pan bolted to the LS1's bottom end.

Tires were long a point of contention. Jim Perkins insisted that the C5 have a spare tire, but Cafaro knew they needed the room, as well as the weight savings afforded by the use of Goodyear's already perfected extended-mobility tires (EMT), or "run-flats" as they had become known since their introduction as a C4 option in 1994. There was even talk of quitting Goodyear—which had supplied Corvette tires since 1978—and trying a Japanese-manufactured tread. Perkins shot this idea down in its tracks—America's sports car would wear American rubber. Goodyear then supplied an even more advanced EMT for the C5.

Cafaro also wanted some seriously large wheels and tires, with the fronts being slightly smaller than the rears to add a rake that would both help aerodynamics and look really cool. One of his models had 17-inch-diameter wheels in front, 19 inches in back. Function, however, quickly took hold of form as the aero-engineering team put a lid on wheel/tire size, which also plays a part in how well a car slices through the wind. Too fat or too big and the C5 wouldn't roll on to that 0.29 Cd.

Although it looked mostly like a C4 Corvette, the CERV IV test vehicle was all C5 beneath the skin. CERV IV was built for $1.2 million in the summer of 1994. David Hill's engineers considered it to be the first of the "alpha" test cars built. Here, CERV IV was caught in December 1997 on display at the National Corvette Museum in Bowling Green.

The gas tank presented its own unique challenge. A conventional shape in the conventional location in back wouldn't do if designers were going to offer any cargo space in the C5. Throw in the rear-mounted transmission and a frame with a large enclosed tunnel running down the middle that intruded into the rearward regions, and the problem appeared unsolvable. Early solutions only created more problems with complicated shapes, too-small sizes, or extra fuel pumps. The final choice was a plastic dual-tank design that straddled the central tunnel and featured connecting lines from side to side. In the beginning it was esti-mated that the complex answer demanded by the gas tank question might add more than $1 million to development costs.

No problem. Not only did it need to be done, but as it was, Hill's engineers reportedly got about half of that back by keeping the frame-rail hydroforming job in-house instead of contracting it out. The lowest outside hydroforming estimate was $1.5 million. GM's own tool and die operation ended up doing the job for well below $1 million. Who'da thunk it?

Victories were certainly plentiful during C5 development. But so were problems—before, during, and

after. Keeping weight down to spec was a full-time job throughout the design process. One of the more interesting solutions to the poundage problem involved using a compartment floor made of balsa wood sandwiched between composite sheets. Along with being lightweight, this construction is 10 times stiffer than composites alone and is an exceptional insulator.

Horsepower was never a worry, but breaking suspension components was, as was calibrating out all the glitches in the various electronic systems and controls. Perfecting production typically tripped up the project. One example involved the first production-line hydroformed rails, which were originally to be delivered March 25, 1994. Problems making the process work, though, pushed that date back a week. GM men did finally get the trick down.

Getting the alpha test car run under way that summer was hindered by various gremlins—parts either weren't showing up on time, or when they did, they sometimes didn't fit. Alcoa Aluminum was also encountering troubles casting the Gen III cylinder blocks, meaning most early alpha cars were going together with iron-block versions.

During testing, some of the plastic gas tanks were found to contain production residues that clogged fuel pickups. That problem was solved simply enough by making sure the tanks were perfectly cleaned out before installation. All other snafus were addressed as well; those mentioned here and many, many more. Hill's gang went over the C5 with a fine tooth comb more than once.

After 1994, all that remained was testing, testing, testing.

The C5 body was not only styled to please the eye, it also had to pass critical wind-tunnel tests. Its stunning 0.29 drag coefficient is literally world class—no comparable sports car anywhere can match that sensational aerodynamic achievement. *Courtesy Chevrolet Motor Division, GM Corporation*

AutoWeek®

October 28, 1996
$2.50 USA $3.50 Canada

Spied!

The new

Corvette

breaks

cover

CHAPTER TWO

CRAWL TO MARKET
The C5 Finally Emerges

It had to happen. Someone had to finally see something. Someone had to finally talk. Someone had to finally listen. In Detroit, very few secrets stay secrets for all that long, either by mistake or plan. The C5 Corvette was no exception. For chrissakes, it took the better part of a decade to bring this car from sketch pad to showroom. Chevrolet couldn't have kept the jackals away forever. Press people wanted to know. The public, as it always has and will, had a right to know. And GM officials knew all along that a little preproduction publicity couldn't hurt anyone.

So some little bird finally sang.

Motor Trend was the first magazine to publish a detailed account of the upcoming all-new Corvette, this in its April 1994 issue. *MT*'s conveniently unsigned piece claimed its facts were "culled from sources within GM and its suppliers." GM insiders figured it was a contractor who spilled the beans, although it really didn't matter. David Hill was happy to see news of the C5 out in public view after working so hard for so long to get it off the ground. John Cafaro was mildly amused by artist Duane Kuchar's accompanying illustration which was close in some ways, yet well behind in others. "Based on educated speculation and show cars like the Sting Ray III, this illustration of the '97 Corvette offers a glimpse into the future of America's greatest sports car," read the caption.

"This is the best information that *Motor Trend* has about the next Corvette," claimed the article. "Some of it is good, solid rumor, some is extrapolation, and some of it is our very finest wild speculation." Wild speculation, huh?

AutoWeek scored the first undisguised photos of the C5 Corvette, courtesy of ace spy photographer Jim Dunne in October 1996, some three months before the car's planned public unveiling. *Used with permission of Crain Communications, Detroit, Michigan*

Motor Trend contributing artist Duane Kuchar created this peek into the future for *MT*'s April 1994 issue. At the time, rumors coming out of GM Design spoke of the next-generation Corvette demonstrating various nostalgic ties to the first Sting Ray. Thus the long, pointed rear glass shown here. *Courtesy Duane Kuchar*

Most of the article was right on. Predictions included a backbone frame, an all-aluminum V-8 measuring about 5.7 liters with probably 1 horsepower per cubic inch, a rear transaxle, round analog gauges, advanced Goodyear run-flat tires, and 18-inch wheels. Other extrapolations were a little off. "We assume the floor pan will be stamped steel. . . . A coil spring front suspension may be adopted. . . . The current Bosch ABS system is apt to be swapped for GM's own Delco design."

Then again, *Motor Trend* was more than willing to shirk some of its obligation to the truth while buttering up its exposed target. "Even if only half of the aforementioned [prediction] proves true, the new Corvette will be well worth the wait."

Perhaps if *Motor Trend* had just waited a bit longer, it wouldn't have missed on the frame, leaving out the hydroformed side rails, or gotten its labels mixed, calling the new V-8 a "Gen 5" while failing to make note of the manufacturer's "C5" designation. Missed as well was the proposed three-car line-up. "Unlike the current Corvette, which was designed initially only as a removable-roof coupe, the next 'Vette is being engineered as both a fixed-roof coupe and an open convertible." At least, thought Russ McLean, there was one secret left, that being the targa-top model. Actually, there were two—the convertible's trunk was also overlooked.

And there remains one last *Motor Trend* prediction yet to be debunked or proven true in early 1998, though it certainly looks like a reach. Citing a "most delicious rumor out of Chevy," the article proposed "that the classic 454-cubic inch big-block V-8 may return to the Corvette as Chevy's response to the 488-cubic inch V-10 Viper." Although reports in late 1997 have mentioned a more powerful V-8 for the upcoming fixed-roof coupe, these claims all point to an even-better-breathing LS1 small-block, not a brutal big-block.

Motor Trend did correct itself in another exposé coming exactly a year later. This time the feature was bylined by Don Sherman, apparently with more than a little help from retired Corvette Chief Engineer Dave McLellan. Almost everything was essentially right on, with the exception of a Joe Goebbel cover illustration that showed exaggerated exhausts and "double bubbles" atop each set of taillights— the latter aspect a design feature already deep-sixed by Cafaro. Sherman also missed the model year, referring to the now correctly identified C5 incorrectly as a 1998 Corvette. His inside contacts also allowed him to put together a third C5 scoop for the September 1996 *Motor Trend*. Included was a specification chart, as well as more Kuchar artwork, now depicting both a coupe and a convertible.

Sherman's April 1995 article had featured more Goebbel art that was amazingly true to life—or maybe not so amazingly. Reportedly, some Polaroids taken of a real C5 inside a GM building showed up anonymously at *Motor Trend*, and these shots were used as a basis for those color renderings.

Also included in Sherman's first C5 feature was a somewhat blurry photo of a disguised C5 credited to automotive spy photographer Hans Lehmann. Lehmann had captured the new Corvette on film at GM's Arizona proving grounds on January 3, 1995. The C5 that Lehmann shot was one of the flat-black alpha cars, this one wearing considerable disguises—a Naugahyde bra up front, a plastic "diaper" in back, and contrasting white lower bodysides. It was rude, crude, and completely uncomplimentary. But it was a real picture of a real C5 Corvette. More importantly, it was the *first* real picture of a real C5 Corvette.

One of many pesky spy photographers who constantly hound supposedly secret cars of the future wherever they go, Lehmann had scooped one of the best, his rival from Michigan, Jim Dunne. In truth, even various amateurs had already managed to trip a shutter on a camouflaged C5 test mule. Dunne scored his first alpha shot early in 1995 in Texas.

The next year he got the last laugh. It was Dunne— the dean of all spy photographers, certainly of all American spy photographers—who in October 1996 snapped the first pro photos of a totally undisguised C5 pilot

Chevrolet built almost 30 beta test cars in 1995, these seeing duty in the heat of the Australian outback and the cold of northern Canada. C5 test vehicles faced temperatures as low as -40 to prove that they could handle every extreme. *Courtesy Chevrolet Motor Division, GM Corporation*

With C5 test vehicle production behind schedule in 1995, David Hill's engineers built 10 to 20 "Cormaros," specially modified Camaros with backbone chassis, rear-mounted transmissions, and Gen III V-8s. Even photographer Jim Dunne was fooled. Notice the fuel filler on the wrong side (directly behind the driver's door) on this Cormaro displayed at the National Corvette Museum.

car (see sidebar, this chapter) this coming some three months before the 1997 Corvette was officially introduced to the world. Dunne's perfectly clean shot of a red C5 coupe landed on *AutoWeek*'s cover the very next day along with the tag, "Spied! The new Corvette breaks cover."

Like the supposedly secret word of the C5 project, it was also only a matter of time before equally secret images of the car began going public against GM intentions—especially so, considering the number of test miles traveled by C5 mules at points across the country and even around the world. According to Hill, his team did at least a half a

CONTINUED ON PAGE 66

Testing demands also forced engineers to use various cleverly modified C4 Corvettes as rolling testbeds. This ZR-1, shown at the National Corvette Museum, was used to perfect the C5 interior (right).

I SPY

Jim Dunne has authored three GM history books. He has been *Popular Mechanics'* Detroit editor for 12 years. And he is one of the most well-known members of the automotive press. But few recognize him for his words. "I've been a writer for 30 years; nobody says anything about that," said Dunne. "But I take a few fuzzy pictures, and all of a sudden, I'm a celebrity."

That he is. Jim Dunne, 66, of Grosse Pointe, Michigan, is a spy photographer, and not just a spy photographer—he's *the* spy photographer. Few, if any in the business do it any better, and none are as feared—and revered—as Dunne. While Detroit officials often feign dismay over his amazing ability to get his scoops, many are not ashamed to admit being honored by his efforts. If anyone's going to steal the shot, it should be the man most famous for doing just that.

Since his first spy gig more than 30 years ago, Dunne has admittedly spent the most time by far lurking around America's sports car. One of his greatest adventures came in 1982 when he rented a helicopter in Death Valley to photograph the C4 Corvette. That effort landed his work on the cover of *Road & Track*.

Dunne's adventurous career began simply enough. His first spy shots—of Chevrolet's remodeled Corvair—came in 1965. He got those, using a borrowed camera, over a fence at GM's Proving Grounds in Milford, Michigan. He then sent them to a New York editor, who said they were "electrifying" and immediately published them. Next, he went out and bought a camera for himself.

Thirty-three years later, his stories are far more—how to put it?—"interesting."

Dunne once exposed more than he bargained for. While on vacation in northern Michigan before the 1974 introduction of the Monte Carlo, he stumbled onto a film crew shooting that new Chevrolet. "They had cameras out, and lights, and executives running around, and models standing around," he remembered. "So I hopped out of my pickup and started taking pictures." Two waving executives only inspired Dunne to step up higher on the running board and continue shooting. "The model then whipped off her wraparound skirt and ran over and held it up in front of the car." Laughed Dunne, "Not only was it exciting, I also got an eyeful."

Another incident involved taking pictures of "bucks"—cobbled-together styling models of new cars—deep in the heart of Pontiac's engineering center. It was during lunchtime when everybody was out. A tense Dunne, worried about getting caught where he shouldn't have been, was photographing three bucks in a row,

When Detroit executives think of spy photographers, one name and one name only comes to mind—Jim Dunne. Dunne, 66, has been doing his covert operations thing for 30 years now. Every day he goes out on a shoot he knows should he ever be caught or killed, his secretary will disavow any knowledge of his actions. *Nick Twork*

Dunne got this first look at a C5 alpha car in Brownsville, Texas, in 1995. It was used for chassis and powertrain testing, and it measured some 9 inches longer than the real thing. *Jim Dunne*

Typically, all alpha and beta cars were heavily disguised so photographers like Dunne couldn't get a clean look. All the excess girth appearing on this alpha came courtesy of various panels, covers, and bras used to hide the C5's true form within. *Jim Dunne*

when up popped the head of a P.R. man over one of the model's backseats. At the same time, a female P.R. aide's head also popped up.

"I took one look at him, turned, and walked out," explained Dunne. "He never reported me, and I never reported him. It was thrilling because I was nailed. I mean, he saw me, but, of course, he was in a compromising position, so what could he say?"

Of course Dunne's fame involves uncovering far more than a stolen moment. He is the man who snapped the first photos of the C5 Corvette fresh

Dunne caught this beta test car at GM's Proving Grounds in Milford, Michigan, in the summer of 1996. *Jim Dunne*

INSET: This sidebar's author models the Corvette T-shirt with its "unauthorized logo" given to her by her close friend Jim Dunne. Dunne amazingly was able to have three of these shirts made in a Bowling Green shop a few months before the new Corvette logo was released to the public.

off the production line in all its uncovered glory, this coming in October 1996. Spy photos had turned up in the press before then. But these were all crude shots of crude cars, Chevrolet's heavily disguised alpha and beta test mules.

After two years of photographing disguised mules in places like Death Valley, the Milford Proving Grounds, and up in Canada, Dunne came to a simple conclusion: "Maybe I could get a better picture if I went down to Bowling Green, Kentucky, where the cars are built. By this time, it was getting close to production, and I knew if I could get one coming out of the factory it wouldn't be covered up like all the others I had shot."

But it wasn't as easy as that. His first day in Bowling Green proved a bust. He could see the car, but it wasn't cover material. So he stayed an extra day. His persistence paid off.

"A red Corvette came out of the factory," he said. "I happened to be in position and got the most beautiful, sharpest, reddest Corvette picture anybody could ever ask for." After a one-hour walk back to his car, he called *AutoWeek* with news of his pictures. But the magazine's October 28 issue was heading to the printer the next afternoon, already wearing a Dunne cover shot, this one a fuzzy photo of a clean, white Corvette. Time was critical. Jim hopped a plane from Louisville to Detroit that evening and delivered his new film to *AutoWeek* first thing the next morning.

"They were ecstatic," he gleamed. "The shots came out beautifully. Red Corvette, lights up, three-quarter front. There was absolutely no disguise on it." *AutoWeek's* cover was then refitted with the red Corvette just in the nick of time. And Jim Dunne was once again "The Man."

GM's reaction to his latest electrifying shoot? "I was congratulated by different people saying, 'we were betting on you; we thought you would be the first one to get it,'" he said. "The people who work on these cars are proud of them; they want the public to see them. Underlining all the resistance to having pictures taken is this idea: GM men want people to see their work. My pictures were just sensational. [GM people] couldn't have asked for better publicity. It ran on a cover. What the hell? They were not upset at all."

Sensational photos weren't the only things Dunne left Bowling Green with that October. The day before his shoot, he stumbled upon a T-shirt factory amazingly advertising the new Corvette logo, a redesign that had yet to go public. Even members of the press hadn't caught a glimpse of it, yet there it was, readily available. A worker told him he could buy a shirt wearing the new logo.

"I'd like a dozen of those Fruit-of-the-Loom T-shirts," ordered Dunne. "I only have three left," she replied. "I'll take all three," he retorted. "Put the logo here."

Dunne then visited the National Corvette Museum across the street from the Corvette plant. "Do you have any T-shirts with the new Corvette logo?" he asked at the boutique counter. "Oh no, we really want those, but we haven't got them yet," came the answer. "We're not allowed to sell them for another month or two."

What a big score in Bowling Green. Jim Dunne left town toting the first C5 photos, three T-shirts with the supposedly unannounced new Corvette logo, and a feather in his cap. And where are those shirts now? "I gave one to my mother, one to my daughter, and one to someone special," Dunne said with a smile in 1998.

—Joyce Tucker

CONTINUED FROM PAGE 62

million road miles putting the C5 through its paces, many millions more in laboratory simulations.

Warm-weather testing was done in Arizona and Death Valley. Teeth-chattering experiments came in North Dakota and as far up as Kapuskasing, Ontario, some 550 miles north of Toronto. And when the weather in our hemisphere wasn't supplying Hill's crew with the conditions they required, they simply went somewhere else. Remember, when it's summer in the northern hemisphere, it's winter in the southern, and vice-versa. In January 1996, two C5s, a beta and a prototype, did 50,000 test miles in the parched outback of Australia while engineers back in Detroit were freezing their pocket protectors off.

The whole alpha/beta idea was a new one at GM, it coming along as part of the equally new Four-Phase process. Before Four-Phase, the corporation had for decades tested its designs using prototypes that were very close to the final product. They were quite refined. The alphas, on the other hand, were rough as cobs in comparison, and intentionally so. The idea was to test parts and designs before they were finalized, letting later vehicles handle all the resulting refinement. Accordingly, what was proven by the alpha cars was used to build better beta machines. In turn, the betas would lead up to true prototype production, which would serve to validate all the lessons learned.

Previously, GM typically built 200–300 prototypes of a given new car. Hill's team intended to do the same type testing with less than 100 C5 counterparts—alphas, betas, and the rest included.

Hill himself first drove the C5's original testbed, the CERV IVa, on the track at GM's Milford Proving Grounds in the summer of 1993, and he loved it. About one year later, Chevrolet's first C5 Corvette, a flat-black alpha, was driven out of the Midsize Car Division building's "Bumper-to-Bumper" assembly area by build chief John Fehlberg on June 26, 1994. Fehlberg's team at Bumper-to-Bumper then continued working day and night to roll out the second alpha on July 13. Powertrain Division got its first alpha in mid-August, two months behind schedule.

Also behind schedule was the aluminum Gen III V-8. Alcoa Aluminum, which was responsible for casting prototype LS1 cylinder blocks, couldn't get the process down. Powertrain Chief Ed Koerner then turned to the Montupet Company in Ontario, the firm that was scheduled to cast the LS1 production run but as yet was not ready to fire things up. Montupet did, however, use a temporary process to at least start supplying some blocks to Koerner for testing. This still took time, and until it all was sorted out, most early alphas were fitted with heavier iron-block versions of the Gen III.

Most of Hill's engineers got their initial experience behind an alpha's wheel at the Arizona proving grounds in January 1995. By then designers back in Detroit had already been thrilled by Bumper-to-Bumper's first alpha, as it had gone into the wind tunnel and come out with a Cd of 0.309—a fantastic base line.

The beta build began on April 10, 1995. On June 20, the first white beta body was dropped onto its backbone chassis, but this came three weeks behind schedule. Slow-in-coming parts supplies and problems with some parts that simply didn't cut it kept both the alpha and beta assembly work from making very important deadlines. Of the latter, 28 betas were eventually built, with 18 of these being fully functional, real-world test machines.

With alpha and beta supplies themselves slow in coming, Hill had to make do with whatever he could get his hands on to accomplish all the testing required to make full production by September 1996. In one case, a C4 ZR-1 was used to explore the C5 interior. Even though it was a screaming yellow zonker, this rolling testbed drew no attention whatsoever to itself on public roads while proving and disproving how well the C5 interior worked in actual dri-

On June 20, 1996, the last C4 Corvette rolled off the Bowling Green assembly line, one day ahead of schedule. On the following day it was presented to noted Corvette collector and parts supplier Mike Yager of Mid America Designs, in Effingham, Illinois. Yager also owns the first C5 Corvette delivered to the public. *Tom Glatch*

The C5 assembly line at the Bowling Green plant finally commenced operation in September 1996. Although it did start up right on deadline, assembly glitches pushed back the build schedule by about a month. *Courtesy Chevrolet Motor Division, GM Corporation*

ving conditions. Other C4 mules were also used to make additional tests that didn't require complete C5 structures.

Hill even went as far as to transform about 10 to 20 1995 Camaros into "Cormaros"—F-bodies on the outside, Y-cars underneath. Central tunnel frame with hydroformed side rails, a rear-mounted transmission, the Gen III V-8—it was all in there somewhat crudely wrapped up in Camaro sheet metal. Built in the spring of 1995, Cormaros also were initially put together with iron-block Gen IIIs. But all were eventually refitted with the aluminum V-8 once it became available. Other modifications included moving the fuel filler to the driver's side. The C5 team used standard Camaros too, these equipped only with the Gen III for specific engine-testing experiments.

Not only did the Cormaro fleet allow engineers to proceed with testing what otherwise would have waited for the arrival of alphas or betas, it also guaranteed that testing could go on in broad daylight without worry of giving away any C5 secrets. Even Jim Dunne was fooled. In the summer of 1995, he caught a Cormaro in Death Valley but misidentified it only as a warmed-over Camaro doing duty as an engineering plaything. For once, the test drivers kept their secret—and got the last laugh.

Hill did so, too. After all those missed deadlines, all those delays and dragging schedules, the C5 Corvette still managed to show up on time for its debut. Almost amazingly, one part of the plan came in ahead of schedule. On June 20, 1996, a white 1996 Corvette coupe, the final C4, rolled off the Bowling Green assembly line one day before intended. And that was one extra day for workers to finish clearing out the old line to bring in the new. By August, parts for the 17 pre-pilot cars—built to train line workers—were arriving at the plant. The last of these cars was still moving down the line on September 3 when the first C5 frame members started finding their way into welding jigs. Almost four years earlier, C5 team leaders in November 1992 had established this exact date as the first day for 1997 Corvette pilot car production. At least they hit the most important deadline right on the nose.

Here, the C5's hydroformed side rails are welded into a frame in a jig at the Bowling Green assembly plant. These one-piece steel sections are die-formed from pre-bent round tubes into rectangular rails using fantastic hydraulic forces. Once sealed and fit between the dies, fluid (mostly water) is pumped in at pressures up to 6,000 psi to literally blow up the tubes to shape. *Courtesy Chevrolet Motor Division, GM Corporation*

But in keeping with the untrustworthy nature of the C5 development tale, that day did not mark the end of frustration and the beginning of a new generation of Corvettes. Problems still wouldn't go away. Problems with substandard parts. Problems with assembly processes. That first frame ended up underneath not a salable pilot car, but a body structure built for more testing, one of three such structures produced. More test cars were built in September, this even though the time for building prototypes was officially over and these should have been pilots. The first pilot car did finally appear on October 1, by which time the snags had been fully ironed out.

Or at least enough to now let the market do all the testing.

CHAPTER THREE

HIGH-FIVE
Celebrating the 1997 Corvette

The automotive press got its first look at the real thing in November 1996. Chevrolet chose to show off its C5 Corvette in a long-lead format broken up into two parts: journalists began the presentation at the Corvette's home in Bowling Green, then were whisked away south for some warmly welcomed drive time at Road Atlanta outside Gainesville, Georgia.

"When reporters finally drove it," said David Hill, "they were probably a little awestruck that the Corvette had been reinvented. And, in fact, there are only a few holdover parts on the car; everything else is new. But that was the intention all along, to make the new Corvette a big surprise, a revolution."

Of course, whatever responses, whatever information the journalists gleaned from this event, was embargoed.

Typically, no one could print anything until after the new Corvette's official introduction to the world scheduled for the turn of the year. It was like trying to keep a really big secret back when you were in first grade.

That long-anticipated intro came January 6, 1997, at the North American International Auto Show in Detroit. And at the exact same time in Los Angeles. With the exact same red Corvette. Honest. Well, at least Chevrolet tricksters, working in concert with professional magician Franz Harary, wanted us to think that was the truth. With cameras rolling at both ends of the show, that red C5 mysteriously disappeared from the stage in Detroit and almost immediately reappeared in L.A. Then it came back East. Once there, it seemingly floated above the stage, suspended by nothing more

The many differences between the 1996 and 1997 Corvettes make them like night and day. Rolling on a longer wheelbase, the C5 is both wider and taller than the C4.

While the C4 body appears larger due to its high beltline, the C5 is actually about an inch taller from roof to ground. The C5 wheelbase was also lengthened more than 8 inches.

The Bowling Green plant's paint booth is fully automated. Robotics handle all spraying chores. The booth is also as close to dust-free as can be imagined. *Courtesy Chevrolet Motor Division, GM Corporation*

than our imaginations. Or theirs. How'd the Bow-Tie guys do it? They'll never tell. But they will say why.

"We couldn't see letting the Corvette out of the stable without a very special send-off," said John Middlebrook. "It's an exciting car. It deserves an exciting first public appearance."

That it did—for so many different reasons.

"The driver in me couldn't be more pleased with the '97 'Vette," said John Heinricy, total vehicle integration director for the C5. "Anyone who has spent a significant amount of time in a Corvette is going to see that we made a big leap forward. We improved ride, handling, comfort, quality, power, and refinement."

The list of those improvements is not only long, it's also heavily cross-referenced; so many changes not only worked on their own but also assisted in various other benefits. Making the car more rigid improved ride and handling. It also made the car more comfortable. Moving the transmission to the rear improved handling as well by helping better balance the C5. It *also* made the car more comfortable. There is now both more room at your feet and more space all around inside the passenger compartment.

The prime mover behind so much of the C5's improvement is that incredibly rugged frame with its center tunnel section and hydroformed side rails. It is 4.5 times more rigid than the C4 frame, which means many things. With so much strength below, the body didn't require a major amount of weight-adding extra structure, something along the lines of the birdcage used beneath the C4's skin. The entire car is so much more rigid, yet it's still 80 pounds lighter than its forerunner. And, as anyone who has ever dropped the hammer on any car knows, less weight immediately equates to quicker acceleration.

Demonstrating that increased rigidity is the C5's natural frequency measurement. With a larger number being better, the 1997 coupe's natural frequency came in at 23 hertz with the targa top latched down, 21.5 hertz with the top off. Compare that to the supposedly battleship-solid Mercedes 500SL's 17-hertz score.

The body is also tougher. Panels are constructed of a flexible sheet-molded compound (SMC) that is markedly improved in the way it resists life's dings and arrows—and rocks, and shopping carts, and the back ends of old pickup trucks. Accidents do happen. But when a C5 is hit in the rear, panel replacement is made much easier thanks to the fact that the rear quarters are bolted in place, not bonded like before.

Interior room and overall stability were improved by a totally new set of dimensions as the four wheels were moved farther out to each corner of the C5 platform. Wheelbase was stretched by 8.3 serious inches to 104.5. Front track was widened 4.3 clicks to 62 inches, while the rear went from 59.1 to 62.1 inches, the same as the fat ZR-1. Total body width in back actually surpasses the old ZR-1 bodyshell by a half inch. Roof height too grew, to 47.7 inches, 1.4 more than before.

What adjustments have these changes made to the Corvette's image? Results are mixed, at least in Jim Dunne's opinion. "Generally, I like the car," he said. "But I do not like the shape, the length of the wheelbase. I had seen unofficial versions of the [C5]. I thought it said, 'I am a Corvette. I am stronger. I am lower. I'm just as dramatic as the old one. But I'm not radically different.'" Then Dunne saw the real thing with its radically lengthened wheelbase. "I love the tighter dimensions on the old [Corvette]; it looks more like a sports car in the traditional sense," he responded. "The wheels are closer; the wheelbase is shorter, and it looks crouched up, ready to spring. The [C5] looks like . . . well, I guess, the difference between a dog running with its four feet together and a dog running with its four feet spread out."

Yet, as much as its longer stride seems to turn off some critics, many still feel the C5's overall impressions are positive. "It does give kind of a longish look directly from the side," Dunne continued. "But a three-quarter front [view] just looks terrific." And the opposite end? "That back end has been criticized, that vertical rear fascia," said Dunne. "I'm kind of used to seeing it now, and it looks better the more I see it. It looked so radical when you first saw it; it wasn't all that appealing. Now it looks good. It looks dramatic. It looks challenging."

Beauty remains, as always, in the eye of the beholder. And the C5 Corvette's shape naturally totally thrills some while disappointing others. But next to no one can deny the attractions beneath the skin. All that extra length, width, and height means drivers can no longer complain about crowded quarters, both for themselves and their luggage.

Much of the C5's redesign process involved listening to and prioritizing such complaints about earlier Corvettes. "The voice of the customer was telling us the car had to be well built," said Jeff Juechter, total vehicle integration engineer. All those shakes, rattles, and squeaks common to the C4 had to be eliminated and were, thanks to the new C5 frame. Of course, the most noticeable benefit of the design is the dropped door sill, 3.7 inches lower than the C4's hurdle-like entrance. Entering and exiting a Corvette has long been an accepted pain, a part of the price paid for driving America's greatest sports car. With those sturdy hydro-formed rails taking up less space beneath the doors, that task is now more short-skirt-friendly.

And the entire car feels more welcoming, more solid, more safe. Responding to earlier complaints has resulted in a long list on its own of improved "human factors," with the dropped step-over height at the door sill being among

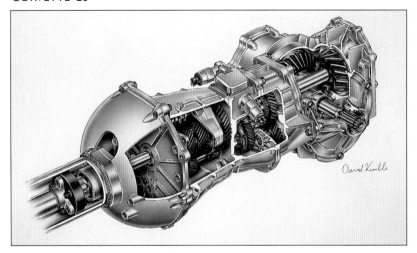

A Borg-Warner T56 six-speed is the manual choice for C5 customers. As usual, the top two gears are overdrives. Notice the torque tube connection at the far left. *Courtesy Chevrolet Motor Division, GM Corporation*

The C5's automatic transmission is an electronically controlled four-speed Hydra-Matic 4L60-E. *Courtesy Chevrolet Motor Division, GM Corporation*

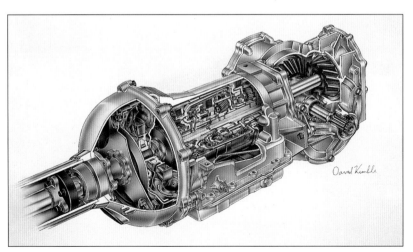

these. Shortening the liftover reach into the cargo bay in the back is another, as is adding 3.1 more inches of legroom to the driver's footwell and a warmly welcomed 6.3 additional inches on the passenger side. Yet another is the way all controls—switches, knobs, handles, etc.—have been maximized as far as location, size, and distance from the driver is concerned. Comfort is not just a matter of interior space and quality ride. And performance doesn't just involve the car alone.

"The teamwork, creative energy, and thoughtfulness that went into the optimization of human factors and harmony is something of which I take great satisfaction," said David Hill. "The layout is arranged to help the driver perform whether in a competitive driving situation or getting home on a snowy night."

Dunne feels Hill has a right to be proud. "One of the contradictions about sports cars is you think they're driven by a person of action," he said. "Whether it's a man or a woman, they're active, athletic people." Thus, as he sees it, past Corvettes were commonly excused for the way they minimized human factors.

But that doesn't mean certain aspects of driving one can be easily overlooked. "You climb into the old Corvette," explained Dunne, "and you sit back like a baby in a baby seat. You're completely helpless. You're just kind of lying there. It's so passive. And then you have to go through contortions to get out. It's not a quick, easy, and out like you would imagine active people would want. The new one solves a lot of that. You can just slip in and out real quickly. [The C5] more fits the image of an active person. Everything seems to come together on this car better than it did on the old one."

In keeping with that newfound harmony, that improved ease of use, the C5's removable targa top no longer requires a ratchet to remove, as was required in the C4. Just flip three latches and store the roof panel in the rear compartment. You don't even need an extra pair of hands. With a lightweight magnesium frame, the composite roof panel retains a good measure of structural

Many C5 owners feel the underside of their cars is prettier than the top, and that's saying an awful lot. All that ribbed aluminum certainly gives the driveline a race car look. So, too, do those belly pan panels, which helped aerodynamic engineers get the car down to the 0.29 Cd.

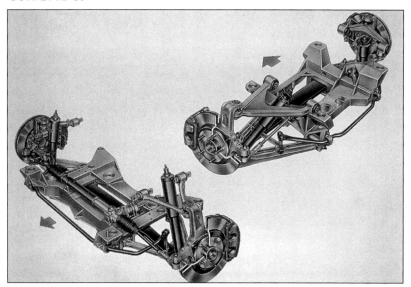

The C5 suspension is fully independent SLA (short-arm, long-arm) at all four corners. Previously, Corvette rear suspensions had a lower control arm but used the half shaft as an upper locating member. A true upper A-arm was added to the C5 rear suspension, shown here on the right. Magnasteer II rack and pinion steering and big four-wheel discs with Bosch ABS are also part of the deal. *Courtesy Chevrolet Motor Division, GM Corporation*

integrity while still tipping the scales farther to the left than its C4 counterpart.

Even more harmony was created inside by adding a much needed dead pedal to that widened driver's side footwell and returning to analog gauges in place of the long scoffed-at digital dashes used since 1984. According to *Motor Trend*, the C5 instruments now "hover in a dazzling ultraviolet glow that gives them uncanny readability and a wow-factor that the digital, Atari-inspired C4 instrument cluster could never match."

When not carrying the top in back, the C5's total cargo space measures at a whopping (for a Corvette) 24.9

The added width of the C5 is plainly evident from a tail view. And the expanse of its rear panel makes the 1997 Corvette appear much larger, compared to its 1996 forerunner, than it actually is.

cubic feet, twice as much as the C4 offered. The C5 not only has the most usable cargo space of any Corvette ever, it easily beats any sports car on the market in this category, although Porsche, Ferrari, and the like undoubtedly couldn't care less. But this is America, and Americans have always preferred to have their cake in both hand and mouth. Contributing to that major cargo space increase is the new frame's layout, the cleverly designed dual fuel tank arrangement, and the deletion of a spare tire.

Omitting the spare tire was made possible by the standard use of Extend Mobility Tires, the "run-flats" that had been offered as a C4 option (RPO WY5) since 1994. With its reinforced sidewall, Goodyear's Eagle F1 GS EMT is able to support the car's weight even when totally deflated at a reasonable speed, say, 50 miles per hour. A flattened EMT can reportedly roll on for as many as 200 miles if that's what you need to find the nearest friendly neighborhood Goodyear dealer. Safer recommendations call for no more than 50 miles on a zero-pressure run-flat to avoid damage to a highly prized tire. So if it works so well, how do you know when a run-flat is flat? Part of the deal is a standard onboard tire pressure monitoring system that keeps the driver informed, to a 1 psi margin of error, of just how much air he or she is rolling on.

Goodyear redesigned its Eagle F1 GS EMT rubber for the new Corvette. The C5 rendition now features a skinnier tread than earlier versions; this a concession to the wind tunnel. Even with a little less tread on the road, the C5 still can brag of better skid pad performance than the C4, 0.93 g, compared to 0.91 for the 1996 Corvette. And don't forget those wind-tunnel results. At 0.29, the C5's drag coefficient is better by far than any American production car and even tops every sports car in the world in Corvette's class.

CONTINUED ON PAGE 83

OF APPLES AND ORANGES

Comparing this country's two best and baddest sporting machines has been one of the fastest games in town since Dodge first dared to challenge the king of the hill seven years ago. And why not? At the price, the brutish, if not savage, Viper surely stands as a certified world-beater in the sports-car ranks. Anything faster requires at least half again as much cash to plop you down into that cozy, even claustrophobic, driver's seat.

The Corvette has never encountered a more able and willing rival than Dodge's sleek, slithering snake. Pretenders to the throne have been few since 1953, and not one has tried to match America's sports car toe-to-toe. Yes, Ford's early two-place Thunderbird was an obvious knock-off, and it did steal a fair share of the six-cylinder Corvette's rumble in 1955. But Dearborn's goal then was to create an entirely different marketplace for an all-new carrot-on-a-stick called "personal luxury." From there, comparisons between T-bird and 'Vette quickly waned.

On the performance field of battle, other intriguing wannabes did appear, albeit briefly. Supercharged Studebakers in the 1950s. Blown Avantis in the 1960s. American Motors' two-seat AMX in 1968. Nice tries, but all were better off staying on their own familiar porches and letting Chevy's really big dog run wherever it wanted.

Not so for Carroll Shelby's Ford-powered, California-built creations, those early GT-350 Mustangs in 1965 and 1966 and his venomous A/C Cobras of 1964 to 1968. Shelby American's crude, seethingly sexy 427 Cobra could certainly take a savage bite out of a big-block Corvette driver's lunch. Nonetheless, Sting Rays continued owning the American road in the 1960s, thanks to, if nothing else, sheer numbers. Twenty-thousand Corvettes a year easily overshadowed the couple hundred Cobras built. And cost, convenience, and class were all clearly in Chevrolet's favor.

Much the same still applies three decades down that road. Sure, Viper and 'Vette are naturally paired rivals; they do ooze sex appeal, and neither suffers from a shortage of performance, raw or refined. And, yes, both do have room for only two riders, hopefully in opposition sexually—dogs may love trucks, but oodles of women will forever fall head over heels for either of these four-wheeled libido mills. All that aside, remaining comparisons appear very much like squaring off apple against orange. First and foremost, 345 horsepower will never equal 450. No matter how you slice it. The same goes for $40,000 and $70,000.

This imbalance has become even more apparent now that the latest, greatest Corvette has taken its turn toward sophistication. Whereas the C5

Like Corvette owners, Viper drivers have had their fair share of complaints concerning the rude ways of the earlier roadsters. Then in 1996 Dodge introduced a coupe version, the GTS. At least now Viper owners have roll-up windows.

is now a kinder, gentler sports car, the Viper remains a wild animal, although Dodge designers have apparently finally opened their suggestion box. Customer complaints involving comfort and convenience were recently addressed, with the results all coming together in the form of the GTS coupe, introduced as a 1996 model.

Like the Corvette in its infancy, the Viper came into this world with little more than the four wheels it rolled in on. In both cases, a sloppy soft-top and side curtains didn't quite cut it with the spoiled sports car crowd on this side of the Atlantic. On top of that, many felt the Viper's original shin-sizzling side pipes weren't too cool. They not only made entry and exit a lot like jumping from the frying pan into the fire, they also didn't do much at all for the way the aluminum V10 announced its presence. According to *AutoWeek's* Matt DeLorenzo, the original Viper roadster sounded like "a UPS truck at idle."

The GTS coupe represented Dodge's stab at sophistication for the Viper. Along with its nicely styled-in hardtop, the Viper coupe also incorporated the breed's first real glass roll-up (electrically) windows, a more socially acceptable feature that then carried over into the roadster's ranks. Although the already cramped passenger compartment was made even more foreboding with the low, fixed roof in place, at least designers managed to allow stature-challenged drivers a better fit behind the wheel. New for the GTS were adjustable foot pedals that could be mechanically moved 4 inches forward and backward. Dual airbags and better-located instruments were also included.

A stiffer platform (thanks to both the added roof and a revised floor pan), numerous suspension upgrades, and a lightened, pumped-up 8.0-liter V-10 (upgraded to the aforementioned 450 horsepower) went beneath that beautiful new body, which was initially done only in blue with white racing stripes—a combo copied off of Shelby's victorious Daytona coupes of 1964. And while the exhausts still travel through the door sills—which still get hot and still wear a warning sticker saying so—they now travel all the way to the Kamm-back tail of the car, where some critics say they release a note more pleasing to the horsepower hound's ears. Sorry, but beneath that flip-up nose, the GTS coupe continues sounding much like the pickup that originally donated those 10 cylinders.

When you boil it all down, Viper and Corvette are two slightly different breeds built for slightly different drivers. Hands down, the Viper is more muscular, just what you might expect from a performance machine priced about 30 grand more. But it's also less friendly, which in turn is just what you might expect from a car brutally bent on being America's most powerful performance machine. Chevrolet's Corvette crew like to think there should be more to it than that. Thus, they sweated the details and refined an already proven performance package. Dodge may have the baddest boy in the valley. But Chevy still has America's sports car.

Those side pipes that singed so many legs on earlier Vipers were deep-sixed in the GTS coupe. Exhausts now travel all the way to the tail. Door sills, however, remain a hot spot as the pipes still make their way underneath.

Dodge's Viper was already firmly established as America's most powerful production car. But Chrysler engineers just had to boost that big 488-cubic-inch-displacement V-8 to 450 horses. Scary.

CONTINUED FROM PAGE 79

Those Goodyear EMTs are mounted on aluminum wheels that, for the first time in Corvette history, differ in diameter front to rear. In front are 17-inchers measuring 8.5 inches wide. In back follow 9.5-inch-wide rims that are 18 inches tall. Tire specs are 245/45ZR17 in front, 275/40ZR18 in back.

Like interior space and ride comfort, the C5's suspension also benefited greatly from the beefed-up frame. With absolutely no unwanted flex left in the chassis, suspension components could be dialed in far more precisely; they no longer have to compensate for ever-so-slightly changing geometry. Mounting points stay put, and the wheels do exactly as engineers planned.

A fully independent SLA (short/long arm) suspension features all-new components. In back, actual upper control arms were added to let the half shafts do the job they're best suited for—transferring torque to the rear wheels. Previously, Corvette's half shafts also served as a locating member in a triangulation layout to help keep the rear wheels in line. Now the rear setup is in parallel. Those upper and lower control arms are made of cast aluminum to save weight, as are the lower arms in front. The upper front arms are forged aluminum.

Transverse-mounted composite leaf springs are used in similar fashion to past Corvettes. These springs, however, feature modified mounts and lower rates, the latter a ride-improving luxury allowed by all that increased platform rigidity.

With these softer springs, the C5 suspension offers an amazing combination of sports car handling and sport sedan ride. This aspect was also enhanced by bushing choice. Front bushings are quite hard in composition to resist cornering loads and keep wheel geometry precise. Rear bushings are softer for more compliance over bumps and jolts. The end result is a performance car that handles the curves like a pro, yet still offers seat-of-the-pants responses of a kinder, gentler nature.

"The far reaching changes to the chassis and suspension have moved the Corvette from the realm of yester-tech to the leading edge of sports car design," wrote *Motor Trend*'s Jeff Karr.

And if the standard C5 suspension wasn't advanced enough, two optional packages are also offered. The F45 Selective Real Time Damping option presents drivers with a choice between three different suspension settings, Tour, Sport, and Performance. As in past adjustable suspension systems, the F45 equipment does this trick by changing shock valving to reduce or increase wheel damping.

At the top of the scale is the ever-present Z51 Performance Handling Package with its stiffer springs, larger shocks, and thicker stabilizer bars. Z51 stabilizers measure 30 millimeters in front, 21.7 millimeters in back. Both the base suspension and the F45 optional setup feature 24-millimeter bars in front, 19.1-millimeter bars in back.

C5 steering is by a revised Magnasteer II system, a variable-effort rack-and-pinion design. Magnasteer II allows lower steering effort at slow speeds for ease of parking, etc. At higher speeds, steering effort goes up for positive road feel and stability. The Magnasteer system has a quick 16:1 ratio. Lock to lock is only 2.66 turns of the wheel.

"We chose to use [Magnasteer] because of the extra preciseness and crispness it gives to the handling of the car, especially in high-performance driving," explained John Heinricy. "It also makes it a lot easier to drive your Corvette in everyday situations."

Brakes are typically four-wheel discs, in this case with larger rotors and special duct work up front to supply cooling air. Rotor measurements are 325x32 millimeters in front, 305x26 millimeters in back. The aluminum calipers are of twin-piston design up front, while single pistons are used in the rear. A Bosch four-channel ABS V antilock system is standard, as is traction control to resist wheel spin. As in the past, the traction control feature can be deactivated by the driver at a touch of a button.

Power comes from the 345-horsepower, 5.7-liter LS1 Gen III V-8—for more on this aluminum pushrod small-block, see the following chapter. Transmission choices are two—the standard, electronically controlled,

Both front and rear tracks have been widened on the C5. Notice the daytime running lights on the 1997 coupe, a feature now found on all GM cars.

The lightweight magnesium-frame targa top comes off much easier than its C4 counterpart. Latches now hold it in place; a ratchet is no longer needed. Even though two able-bodied riders are shown here doing the job, either one of them could've accomplished the task on their own.

As was the case with the C4's top, the C5's removable roof panel stores easily beneath the lift-up rear glass. Two spring latches hold it in place.

four-speed 4L60-E Hydra-Matic automatic and the Borg-Warner T56 six-speed manual. In the 4L60-E's case, the torque converter is mounted in a typical bell-housing adjoining the rear-mounted transmission's two-piece aluminum case. The clutch for the Borg-Warner box stays with the LS1 up front. First gear for the six-speed is 2.66:1, 3.06 for the automatic.

The interior design team turned back to analog gauges to finally squelch all the jokes previously aimed at the C4's digital instrument panels. The C5 dash lights up at night in an eerie 3-D type effect. *Courtesy Chevrolet Motor Division, GM Corporation*

With either choice, an aluminum torque tube ties engine and transmission together and houses a metal-composite driveshaft. A Gertrag limited-slip transaxle completes the drivetrain. Axle ratios are 3.42:1 for the T56, 2.73:1 for the Hydra-Matic. Automatic trans drivers can also opt for a 3.15:1 rear gear.

All this and for a base price of about $39,000. For that money a C5 Corvette driver gets 0–60 in 4.7 seconds, quarter-mile performance of 13.36 seconds at 109.4 miles per hour, and a top end just that side of 170 miles per hour. On the flip side, braking from 60 miles per hour to rest requires only 125 feet.

Throw in estimated fuel economy of 18 city, 28 highway (for the manual trans), and you begin to finally get the picture.

Motor Trend called it "the first-ever no excuses 'Vette," an apt description. The C5 Corvette does so many different things so well it's easy to forget it's a sports car. But that it is. As *Sports Car International* D. Randy Riggs explained, "At $40,000 you can't beat it for handling, acceleration, top-speed—all the things we love in a sports car."

And that's not just *a* sports car. That's America's sports car. The best yet.

CHAPTER FOUR

A FRESH SHEET OF PAPER
Corvette's LS1 V-8

Looking at the C5 Corvette's totally redesigned Gen III LS1 V-8, we can almost get a feel for the thrill Chevrolet followers experienced when that first hot little small-block hit the streets in 1955. Chevy drivers haven't looked back since. And Corvette drivers can thank their lucky stars that that simple, wonderfully adaptive powerplant—the division's first modern overhead-valve V-8—did appear when it did. If it hadn't, this proud 45-year legacy we're all paying homage to now might never have survived past 1954.

So it is today that the Corvette's engine carries on in a proud tradition every bit as significant as the car it powers. As a 1996 factory press release explained, "Based on a timeless design by former Chevrolet Chief Engineer Ed Cole, the 'Gen III' 5.7-liter V-8 marks a bright new chapter in the highly respected lineage that GM small-blocks have established in more than 40 years." 265, 283, 327, 350—each of these lively V-8s has made a name for itself beneath a forward-hinged fiberglass hood. L-84, L-79, LT-1, L98, the other LT1, LT4. No one can deny that Chevy's tireless small-block legacy probably stands as the most storied in American powertrain history. But to say that the LS1 represents a "bright new chapter" is selling the Gen III breed a little short. Or a lot.

More fairly, the LS1 story is an epic tale all to itself. First, it shares a family tree with previous Chevy small-blocks in name alone. Even the extensively modernized Gen II V-8, which debuted in 300-horsepower LT1 form in 1992, can't hold a candle to the length and breadth of the Gen III's list of break-from-tradition innovations. Yes, the

---

When the Corvette was born, it was powered by Chevy's revered "Stovebolt" six, albeit the Blue Flame rendition. Forty-five years later, two more cylinders and a whole boatload of technological lessons learned have resulted in the best Corvette V-8 yet, the LS1.

89

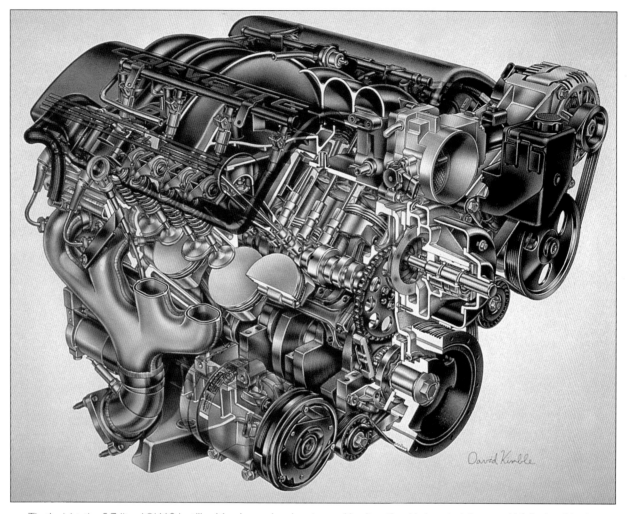

That's right, the 5.7-liter LS1 V-8 is still a 16-valve pushrod motor, making it noticeably low-tech in a world full of multi-valve DOHC engines. But its 345 horses easily make up for its apparently antiquated nature. *Courtesy Chevrolet Motor Division, GM Corporation*

LS1 is a pushrod, 16-valve V-8, just like all Bow-Tie small-blocks since their birth in 1955. And its cylinder block also shares the same time-honored 4.40-inch bore center. From there, though, all bets are off. Engineers even rearranged the familiar 1-8-4-3-6-5-7-2 firing order to 1-8-7-2-6-5-4-3, this to reduce vibration and increase idle smoothness.

At the other end of the tach, the LS1 makes 345 maximum net horses at 5,600 rpm. The 1996 LT4 produced 330 horsepower at 5,800 revs. LS1 torque output is 350 pounds-feet at 4,400 rpm, compared to the LT4's 340 pounds-feet at 4,500 rpm. The base LT1 in 1996 made its 300 horsepower at 5,000 rpm and 335 pounds-feet of torque at 3,600 turns.

What about that 5.7-liter displacement figure you say? Granted, the C4's LT1 and LT4 350-cubic inch V-8s did wear that same hat. That number, however, exists purely out of convenience. In actuality, the LS1's 5.665-liter displacement more specifically translates into 345.69 cubic inches; with bore and stroke numbers rounded off to the tenth, that measurement comes closer to the 347-cubic inch tag commonly bandied about by those of us who still prefer to just say no to metrics. When pressed, Chevrolet does spec the engine at 346 cubic inches.

Furthermore, to fill out those 5.7 liters, the LS1 relies on a revised bore/stroke relationship. Compared to the LT1, the Gen III V-8's bore is less; its stroke is more, this adjustment made to allow more cooling space between skinnier cylinders. Gen II measurements were 4.00 inches for bore, 3.48 for stroke. Speaking of cooling, contrary to the Gen II's reverse-flow system, the Gen III reverts to a conventional design; coolant is once again pumped into the block first, then to the heads.

Undoubtedly most notable among the LS1's innovations is its lightweight yet durable all-aluminum construction, a first for a regular-production Chevrolet small-block and an achievement—like the car it goes into—long in coming. Gen III development had really got cooking in 1993, with the first test engines hitting the dynos at General Motors Powertrain Division that winter. Real-world

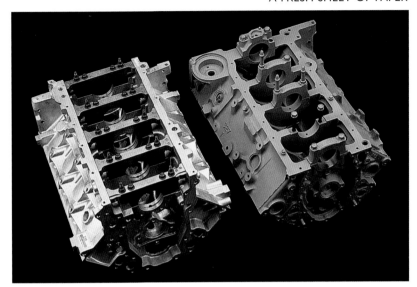

LS1 cylinder heads and block are aluminum, with the latter—shown here on the left in comparison to the previously used LT1 block—featuring a unique deep-skirt design. The lower reaches of the block extend down well below the crank centerline, allowing the main bearing caps to be cross-bolted through that skirt. *Courtesy Chevrolet Motor Division, GM Corporation*

The LS1's aluminum heads feature replicated ports—each one is identical to the next. This was done to maximize flow. *Courtesy Chevrolet Motor Division, GM Corporation*

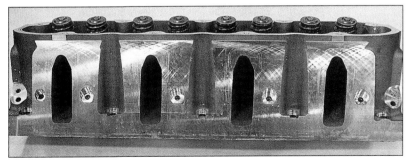

From left to right are the LS1 piston, the LT4 piston, and the LT1 piston. The LS1 aluminum piston is lighter than the other two, and its top ring has been moved up 1.5 millimeters. *Courtesy Chevrolet Motor Division, GM Corporation*

RIGHT: With its dress-up covers removed, the LS1 valve covers reveal the engine's unique ignition system. Each cylinder has its own coil right on top. Ignition voltage only needs to travel through a short wire to the spark plug.

thrashing in alpha cars began the following summer, mostly using prototype iron-block Gen IIIs since aluminum component supplies had yet to materialize. By the time the last beta cars were being complete in late 1995, most of these had been fitted with aluminum Gen IIIs.

Chevrolet engineers officially introduced the Gen III V-8 to the press at three locations across the country in June 1996. By then, the LS1 had undergone every test known to man, from seemingly endless high-rpm durability runs, to searing desert heat exposure, to frigid torture tours in the great white north. During testing in 40-below-zero weather in Kapuskasing, Ontario, the amazing LS1 instantly proved to be an excellent cold-starting engine. Fuel pressure consistencies, throttle workings, and air-conditioning interaction were tested in the 112-degree heat of Death Valley, California.

Out of the car, two Gen III V-8s were run on dyno stands at full throttle for 50 hours with no complaints. Although that achievement met GM specifications, Gen III Chief Engineer Ed Koerner was not convinced; he raised the bar to 260 hours for two more LS1s, then 520 for a single engine. When torn down after its dizzying run, that latter V-8 reportedly looked like new inside.

On the outside, the LS1 shows off its newness in various ways. Another first (for GM gasoline engines) is its "drive-by-wire" electronic throttle control (ETC), which is linked to the traction control and antilock brake systems.

While ETC does simplify the throttle-body/accelerator-pedal relationship (no need to worry about where to route a mechanical linkage in tight quarters), its true goal was to supply more precise throttle response. Little does a driver know that when her foot depresses the right pedal, power, traction, and braking all are being instantly tailored electronically to road conditions, engine status, and the level of performance then being sought from behind the wheel.

Yet, as much as the ETC technology smacks of aerospace influences, the LS1's basic layout remains paradoxically down to earth. For good reasons. "Trying to decide what was the right engine technology for the application was probably the biggest hurdle we faced," explained LS1 Project Manager John Juriga during the Gen III V-8's press introduction in 1996.

Of course David Hill did consider a state-of-the-art overhead cam, multi-valve engine. Hell, why not? Corvette planners had already tried the trick once before with the 1990–1995 ZR-1 Corvette's DOHC, four-valve LT5 V-8. Being a former Cadillac man, Hill was especially fond of the high-tech, 32-valve Northstar V-8. But DOHC engines will always be larger, costlier, and more complicated than their pushrod cousins.

According to Juriga, one plain truth influenced engineering's decision—the C5 engine had to make mucho horsepower while taking up less space than a DOHC V-8. Although his engineers managed to steer him away from the

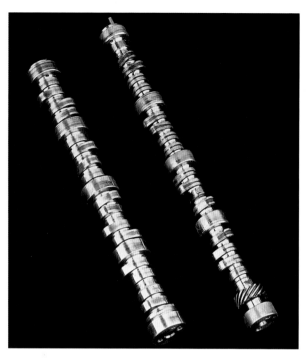

The more stout LS1 cam is obviously on the left here. Cam lobes have enlarged centers to reduce the "ramp" a lifter travels up during the reciprocating process. *Courtesy Chevrolet Motor Division, GM Corporation*

DOHC idea, Hill still kept it in mind until advancing design parameters finally ruled out the possibility of installing such a massive V-8 beneath the C5's low, sloping hood.

Even if size constraints hadn't forced their hand, Koerner's engineers still faced other deciding factors, with pricing being the most prominent. Chevrolet certainly didn't want to see the C5 end up in the sticker stratosphere, where the sky-high-priced ZR-1 had hovered until its eventual demise. Besides, who needed all that extra cost-adding techno-wizardry when Chevy engineers still had a few tricks up their sleeves concerning the supposedly obsolete pushrod V-8?

"The new LS1 has the simplicity and compactness of the pushrod layout, but with porting so efficient and valvetrain so light and stiff, it breathes like an overhead cam motor," bragged Hill about the final product of that engineering magic. "The LS1 is the only engine in the

Corvette for 1997," added Juriga. "We think a base engine at 345 net horsepower is plenty of power. If that can be done with 1 cam, 16 pushrods, and 2 valves in each hole, we can live with that." So can C5 buyers who don't mind at all receiving Porsche performance at a Chevrolet price.

What they get under the hood for that price is a pushrod V-8 that is hardly obsolete. And simplicity in this case is a relative term. Everything about the LS1 was finely engineered to the limit within the parameters set down, beginning with the cast-aluminum cylinder block, which is as tough as they come—and was originally tough to produce.

"Overhead-cam engines are simple from a block standpoint," explained Juriga. "The Gen III," he continued, "made for a complicated block design. The deep skirt, six-bolt bearing caps, deep-threaded head bolt holes, camshaft and tappet locations, and other features made it challenging to engineer."

The points Juriga spoke of involved durability. Weighing only 107 pounds, the LS1 cylinder block tips the scales at 53 pounds less than its Gen II predecessor; the entire engine is 88 pounds lighter. This block is at the same time stronger, thanks to extensive external stiffening ribs and that deep-skirt construction. Unlike typical V-8 cylinder blocks that end at the crankshaft's centerline, the LS1 block extends below the main bearing caps, encasing the crank in a girdle of aluminum that helps hold things together with a vengeance on the bottom end.

That extended skirt also made it possible to cross-bolt the main bearing caps for additional rigidity—thus the six-bolt bearing caps, four in the conventional vertical location on each side of the crank and one each running through the skirt horizontally into each side of the cap. The crankshaft held firmly in place by those caps is cast of nodular iron. For added strength, that crank has rolled-fillet journals, an idea that debuted within the LT4 in 1996. Connecting rods are sintered forged steel, or "powdered metal," another technology introduced in 1996. Cap screws, instead of typical bolts, attach those eight rods to the crank on the big end. At the top, they wear lightened cast-aluminum pistons that squeeze the fuel/air mixture to a 10.2:1 ratio.

Cast from 390 aluminum, heat-treated to the T5 specification, the LS1 block is created by a semi-permanent mold technique that Juriga described as "a cross between diecasting and sand casting." Fitted into the bores are centrifugally-cast, gray-iron cylinder liners.

Cylinder heads are sand-cast, 356-aluminum pieces heat-treated to the T6 spec. Held down by only four bolts instead of the five used by the Gen II V-8, the LS1 heads resist distortion much better, which in turn guarantees a more confident seal against the block deck. Structural integrity was preserved by threading those four bolts deep down into the block, a practice made possible by its deep-skirt design.

Head design is a key to the way the LS1 makes those 345 horses with such ease. Flow wizard Ron Sperry, who joined General Motors Powertrain Division in late 1987, is the man behind the magic in this case. It was Sperry who did the LT1 head in 1992 and its improved LT4 successor four years later.

Much of Sperry's success involved what GM calls "replicated ports." Previous small-block ports were "siamesed" in that they were located in two closely squeezed pairs on the intake side. This meant that the ports varied widely in structure—bending and turning differently with differing volumes—and thus their flow characteristics also varied. Keeping flow rates constant from cylinder to cylinder is an important component of the maximum-performance equation.

The LS1's replicated ports are identical all around—size, angle, spacing, etc.—and run almost uninterrupted as straight as possible to the intake valves. "We worked hard to make sure we had all eight cylinders as close to being identical, from a geometry standpoint, as we could," explained Sperry in 1996. "Each port is a continuous runner-to-valve configuration. We don't have the air turning right or left to any significant degree. There is a relatively large runner opening, and it tapers down so that as the mixture gains

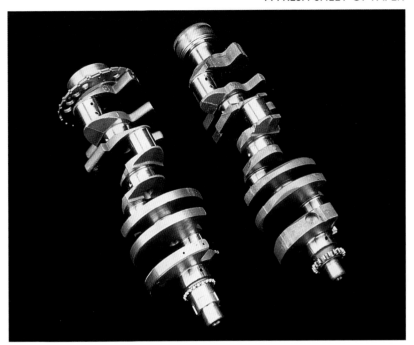

speed, it's also gaining directional stability such that the air is moving toward the valve in a very directed manner. We get the air and fuel into the cylinder with the same level of energy from bank-to-bank and port-to-port."

Also helping maximize flow is the valve angle of only 15 degrees. Valve angle is the measured offset of the valve stem centerline compared to the cylinder bore centerline. A lesser angle means the mixture is flowing more directly into the combustion chamber with less of a bend, less restriction. Consider that a NASCAR Chevy engine has a valve angle of 18 degrees, the Gen II V-8, 23.

Actuating those valves is a steel-billet camshaft that has been rifle-drilled to cut mass. Cam lobes are lower, and their base circles are larger compared to the Gen II design, which means lifters, pushrods, rocker arms, and valves are not subjected to as much acceleration during the reciprocating process; the

The LS1 crank (right) is shorter than the LT1 unit and features some seriously sized journals. Courtesy Chevrolet Motor Division, GM Corporation

One guess as to which main bearing cap is the LS1's. Obviously beefier by far, the LS1 cap uses six bolts, four in the conventional location, two more that work horizontally through the block skirt. *Courtesy Chevrolet Motor Division, GM Corporation*

lifter's trip up and down each lobe is not as steep. And less valvetrain acceleration in turn meant these components could be of reduced mass, which then allowed the installation of lower-tension valve springs. All this adds up to a lessened impact whenever a valve closes on its seat, and that, friends, translates into quieter

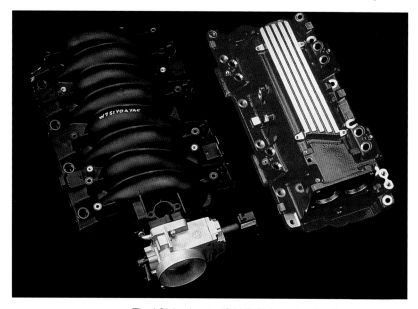

The LS1 intake manifold (left) is made of a plastic material; it is incredibly light, much more so than an aluminum intake could ever be. On the right is the LT4 manifold from 1996. *Courtesy Chevrolet Motor Division, GM Corporation*

valvetrain operation, a big priority in the Gen III design process according to Juriga.

If you're wondering how the LS1 delivers more horsepower than the LT4 with a less lumpy cam, ample valve lift was retained by using higher-ratio rocker arms, 1.7:1, versus the LT4's 1.65:1. Intake lift is 0.472 inch and exhaust is 0.479. LT4 numbers were 0.476 and 0.479. Intake valves measure 2.00 inches, exhaust valves 1.55. Like its roller rockers, the LS1's hydraulic lifters are also of the friction-resistant roller type and are made of cast steel instead of aluminum.

Valvetrain operation is also assisted by its "inline" layout; that is, the centerlines running up the lifters and pushrods and down the valve stems are parallel; previous small-blocks had them at acute angles, which induced side loading whenever a part was pushed in a direction not exactly identical to the part doing the pushing. This inline arrangement reduced friction by doing away with that side loading.

On top, the LS1's sequential electronic port fuel injection is nothing new, working much like similar setups used on Corvettes since 1994: a mass-air-flow sensor meters the incoming atmosphere, and a powertrain control module handles fuel-deliver chores through eight AC/Delco injectors. Newness begins at the intake manifold, which features specially tuned intake runners (15 inches in length for top-end power) and is manufactured out of Dupont's "Nylon 66," a glass-fiber reinforced nylon composite. Benefits of this material are many compared to typically used aluminum; it's lighter, runs cooler, and is easier to manufacture into complicated designs.

Even more intriguing on the bottom end is the "batwing" oil pan, a very flat unit with extended sumps on both sides. You guessed it, those two sumps look like wings. As the story goes, the initial LS1 design called for a shallow pan to fit the C5's restrictive engine compartment. Then, during testing in 1995, an inherent oiling problem was uncovered. Thanks to a high oil level near the crank (due to the pan's shallowness) working in concert with those big bearing caps bridged between the block's deep skirt, the

LS1's lower end was unintentionally divided into four "bays" where air pressure created as each piston went up and down could not move freely—it was trapped between the bearing caps by the oil's surface. With no relief in sight, that pressure aerated the oil supply, foaming it, which then restricted its return drain down from the top end. Additionally, high lateral acceleration sloshed the oil centrifugally away from the pump pickup, inviting failure while the new Gerotor pump was sucking air.

Solutions involved revising the block's lower end to allow that unwanted pressure to escape between "bays." And special baffles and trap doors were added inside a new pan that also increased oil supply from four quarts to six by incorporating those bat-wing sump extensions. To top it off, the bottom end is also reinforced with the pan bolted in place; it's actually a structural member of the engine.

Back topside, the LS1 gets its spark from a distributorless ignition system similar to the design Chevrolet introduced in 1990. What sets this system apart is its one-coil-for-each-cylinder layout. Atop every cylinder, mounted beneath a stylish plastic shield on each valve cover, are eight individual coil and coil driver assemblies tied to their appropriate spark plugs by eight short plug wires. These short wires mean much less energy will dissipate during the voltage's quick journey from coil to plug. An added benefit is reduced radio frequency interference with the car's computers and stereo systems.

Once that hot spark does its job, spent gases are sped out through Ron Sperry's free-flowing exhaust ports into a pair of unique exhaust manifolds designed especially to reduce cold-running emissions. A car's worst emissions are released when the engine is just started. They decrease as exhaust gases heat up the catalytic converter and it starts doing its job. Corvette engineers attacked this problem with a double-walled, hydroformed, tubular exhaust manifold. This design features one welded-up stainless steel tube inside the other, with the air pocket between the tubes' walls serving as an insulator. Whereas typical cast-iron manifolds dissipate heat rather quickly, allowing

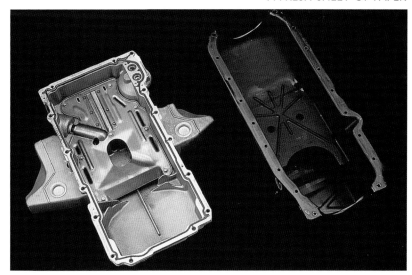

exhaust gases to cool slightly on the way to the catalytic converter, the LS1's "insulated" double-walled manifolds retain that heat, meaning the converter warms up more rapidly. Presto. The LS1 runs as clean as it does hot.

The remainder of the C5's true dual exhaust system incorporates twin catalytic converters, aluminized stainless-steel pipes, dual transverse-mounted, reverse-flow mufflers, and quad exhaust tips. Not all Corvette buyers have been sold on that latter feature, at least from an appearance standpoint. Common curbside comments have ranged from "wimpy" to "silly." As Car and Driver's Csaba Csere saw it in 1998, "just about everyone [on staff] agreed that some sort of shiny, gleaming exhaust pipes would enhance the rear view of the car."

No worry, though. As it always has and always will, the aftermarket parts industry quickly came to the rescue with more than one set of replacement pipes that not only help better dramatize rearward impressions but also reportedly release a few more restricted ponies. The choice is yours.

As for the rest of the LS1 assembly, it would be tough to find another complaint. If this isn't by far the best Corvette engine yet, we'll eat this book.

Differences are also clearly evident on the bottom ends. The LS1 oil pan (left) features sump wings for added capacity; they are needed since lower end clearance mandated a very shallow pan. The LS1 pan also serves as a structural member for the block's lower end. *Courtesy Chevrolet Motor Division, GM Corporation*

CHAPTER FIVE

ALL IS WELL
A Corvette Convertible Returns

"All Corvettes Are Red," at least according to author James Schefter. As he explained it, this claim, which he chose as the title for his in-depth Simon & Schuster-published tale of the C5's conception and birth, came from John Heinricy, at the time head of Corvette development test drivers. "All Corvettes are red," said Heinricy first in the early 1990s. "The rest are mistakes."

In many opinions the same applies to coupes. That is, they are the mistakes. Along with being nothing but crimson in color, all Corvettes should be convertibles. After all, isn't the name America's *sports car?*

In the beginning, all Corvettes were convertibles—with no exception from 1953 to 1955. Before 1962, if you wanted to sissify your Corvette you could have ordered the optional latch-on hardtop, introduced in 1956 as both a conciliation to American sensibilities and a pacification for complaints about the early car's often-leaky top. As *Motor Trend's* Don MacDonald explained it in 1953, apparently Chevrolet's "conception of the Corvette market is that no owner will be caught in the rain without a spare Cadillac."

Then along came the stunning Sting Ray and its stunning hardtop bodyshell. Faced with a choice between coupe and convertible beginning in 1963, most Corvette buyers still favored the open-air style—until 1969. Coupe sales finally took over that year and never looked back. Chevrolet eventually gave up on the Corvette convertible after 1975.

A droptop model did return in 1986, but its popularity never has made it back to earlier levels. In 1996, C4 convertible production was only 4,369, or about 20 percent of the total run. Of course, no convertible was offered

The C5 Corvette may have been designed from the outset as a convertible; nonetheless, it was the coupe that appeared first in 1997, leaving the truly sexy topless model to debut in 1998.

CORVETTE C5

NEAR RIGHT: Operating the C-5's manual top (shown here in reverse to demonstrate the tonneau cover release) is a cinch thanks to its light weight. To put the top up, simply find the release button and lift up the tonneau.

Operating a C4 requires finding the same button beneath the rear cover. If the top was coming down, the driver would also have to locate the release for the two latches (twin dark openings you see on the lid) that hold down the top's trailing edge.

OPPOSITE LEFT: The five-bow top literally raises itself out of its storage bin. It must come out far enough to allow the rear half to accordion up onto itself.

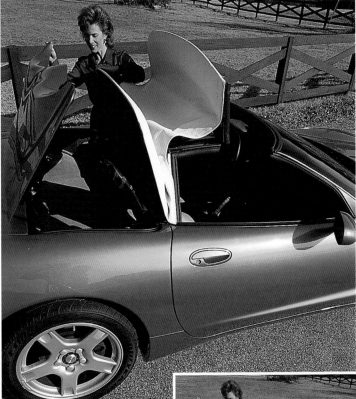

Playing that accordion allows room enough to close the tonneau cover back down.

LEFT: Clearly larger, the C4 top is also noticeably heavier, and unfolding requires a little more effort.

The extra required effort especially comes into play when you're trying to flip up the roof's trailing edge to close the rear cover back down.

Shown here is an additional step that C4 convertible owners have to deal with—the latch for the back end of the folding roof. Reaching under the deck cover and finding this release, along with the yellow release button to its right, was required to start the C4 top-drop process. Since the C5 roof seals itself to its tonneau cover without any latches, a 1998 convertible driver needs only to find one release behind the seat, not two.

ABOVE: Pushing the top down onto the windshield header mechanically flexes the rear half of the top down tight onto the rear deck. Flip two finger latches, and you're done. Reversing the process is, of course, just as light and easy.

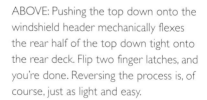

LEFT: Finishing the job on a C4 is akin to closing a car door. The trailing edge of the roof has to be firmly latched in place, something the C5 droptop operator now doesn't have to worry about.

during the C5's debut year of 1997, yet everyone knew it was only a matter of time.

That time came in 1998, to the delight of sun-worshippers and sports-car fans alike. And Corvette people who know how things should be.

"The Corvette convertible is almost an entity unto itself in terms of its following," said Corvette Brand Manager Dick Almond. "Ragtop people are different. They're the type of people who place open-air touring high on their list of worldly pleasures. And since Corvette started life as a convertible, this new convertible is a purist's Corvette."

Witnesses who thought the C5 coupe was big news in 1997 found themselves caught in a double take in 1998. Even Chief Engineer David Hill encountered a little déjà vu. "Like the coupe," he said, "this is the best 'Vette yet." Members of the fourth estate couldn't have agreed more. Calling the new convertible "the most desirable Vette since 1967," *Car and Driver*'s Csaba Csere announced that "not even the glorious ZR-1 models had as many of our staffers muttering about owning a Corvette as does this new roadster."

New is once again the key word. Corvette owners have never seen anything else even remotely like it, nor has any other breed of topless driver for that matter. No other convertible in Corvette history can stand up to the C5 rendition in the way it stands up to the real-world realities of skin-to-the-wind automotive travel.

Sawing the roof off a Corvette, off any car, has always represented a compromise as a coupe's top has always played a major roll in the whole structural rigidity game. Putting it on the bench has always meant additional replacements had to go in, these being frame and cowl braces. Such bracing does help, but most convertibles from the beginning of time still did not measure up as solidly as full-roofed models. In the Corvette's case, cowl shakes, steering wheel vibrations, and general roughness, rattles, and rumbles have always been a part of a convertible's standard features.

Additionally, all that extra structural bracing has, does, and forever will help a convertible put on more than a few unwanted pounds. And due to this weight handicap, droptop muscle machines have all been slower than their coupe counterparts. Inherent realities of convertible ownership have always included less performance and more annoyance.

Not so now.

As earth-shakingly rigid as the coupe is, you must remember that the C5 Corvette was designed first as a convertible, with the goal being to make the platform as strong as it possibly could be even without a top tying it all together. Burning the midnight oil produced that innovative tunnel-section frame with its hydroformed side rails, a unit measuring 450 percent stiffer than the C4 frame. The 1997 C5 coupe obviously benefited tremendously from this work and gained even more strength with its targa-top structure. In the 1998 convertible's case, the beefed-like-a-battleship results were obviously worth the extra sweat.

"It was critical that we didn't just take the coupe and chop off the top to make a convertible," said David Hill. "Corvette's structure has been designed to achieve world-class open-car stability and strength."

That it has. "The C5 convertible's chassis and body is built like Arnold Schwarzenegger's, but without the abdominal ripples," claimed Dain Gingerelli of *Sports Car International*. Beneath that smooth skin is a skeleton that simply refuses to bend or flex. Cowl shake and other common convertible maladies have been virtually eliminated, this without a single extra brace or frame member or any additional weight. Amazingly, the new Corvette convertible, at 3,246 pounds, tips the curb weight scales at only 1 pound more than the coupe—16 ounces. On top of that, the C5 convertible is 114 pounds lighter than its 1996 C4 forerunner.

According to engineers, the convertible at most only measures 10 percent less torsionally rigid compared to the coupe with its targa top on and latched down. Its natural frequency measures at 21.3 hertz, only 2.0 hertz less than the coupe. Compare this to the exceptionally solid Mercedes 500SL, which comes in at 17.0 hertz. The C5 convertible is so rigid it can be equipped with the tough Z51

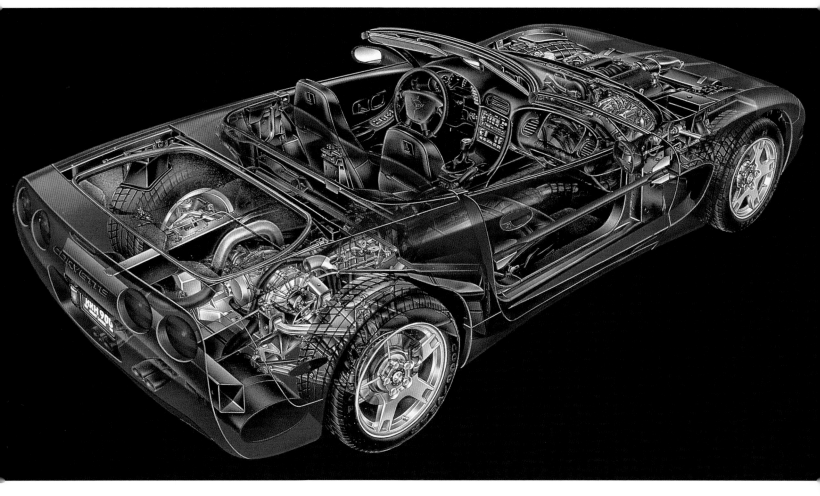

This ghost view shows just how much the tightly packaged chassis layout helps give the C5 convertible so much storage space. And with the top up, this car still manages a 0.32 drag coefficient, only 0.03 less than the wind-cheating coupe.
Courtesy Chevrolet Motor Division, GM Corporation

suspension package, an option that couldn't be offered to C4 convertible buyers. The less solid C4 frame and hard-as-nails Z51 handling equipment just didn't mix.

Apparently neither do the C5 and a roll bar. A rollover hoop, much like the type used by the much more expensive 500SL, also was considered for the 1998 Corvette convertible. But, according to David Hill, observed customer indifference and design complications ruled it out of the C5 plan.

Also ruled out was a power-operated convertible top. Like the C4, the C5's folding roof requires two hands, not just one finger, to put it in its place. As Hill explained, the reasoning behind the choice was simple: keep costs down and available storage space up. As it is, the C5's top folds up so quick- and easy-like, to complain about the lack of power operation only identifies the complainer as being much too lazy to get up out of the seat. At most, to step out and drop the top only takes about 30 seconds off the end of your life. Besides, we could all use the exercise.

Simple, lightweight operation, along with a tight seal when up and an equally tight fit when down, were targets of Chevrolet designers. They penciled out what they wanted, then turned to Dura Convertible Systems, Inc., to try to decipher their scrawls. The job, as one Dura Systems employee reportedly put it, was "like stuffing 10 pounds of bricks into a 5-pound bag."

The result was an articulating, five-bow, pressurized top, pressurized in that when it is unfolded a special linkage in the rearmost fifth bow both squeezes itself down tight against the body and pushes the first four bows upward toward the windshield header where traditional latches make the seal. Pressure in back is so strong no latching mechanism is required to complete what amounts to a superior seal. All this and it's also 1.2 kilograms lighter than the C4 design.

When up, it's still quite aerodynamic as well. The C5 droptop drag coefficient, at 0.32, is only 0.03 higher than the wind-cheating coupe. The 1998 convertible also only loses 0.20 inches of headroom compared to the coupe.

And if you were wondering just how well the top performs in the wind, Hill claims it was tested up to 170 miles per hour and dealt with sustained 150-mile-per-hour runs without any "major ballooning."

When down, the C5 top stows beneath a wonderfully styled tonneau that recalls high-flying Corvette racers from earlier days. More importantly, the tonneau's double-hump headrest fairings allowed designers just that much more room below to hide the top. Thank heavens for those fairings; every extra cubic inch of volume helped. Once folded, the compact C5 top rests in one helluva tight area, all the better to preserve precious storage space in the new convertible's trunk.

That's right, a trunk. Thirty-six years after a Corvette last brought up its rear with real cargo space, the C5 has now resurrected yet another proud tradition—that is to have your cake and transport it in the back of your Corvette convertible, too.

The clever dual-compartment gas tank, deletion of a spare tire (by making "run-flat" tires standard), and the compact, non-power aspects of that folding top all worked in concert to make a trunk possible. And adding a trunk into the C5 equation was yet another way designers could make the new Corvette more user friendly, more practical, more appealing to the modern car buyer. Or more of, as Chevrolet put it, "a practical option for busy Americans and their active lifestyles."

Drivers of rival topless two-seaters can only watch and wish while a C5 convertible drives away with their hopes and dreams of taking anything more than their toothbrush along on a long trip. Porsche 911 Carrera Cabriolet. Forget it, Hans. BMW Z3 six-cylinder. You too, Biff. Viper RT/10. Tough torque-wrenches, Rocky.

Keeping things all in the family, the 1998 convertible welcomes travelers with twice the cargo volume of its 1996 forerunner, that with the top up. With their tops down, the C5 beats the C4 four to one. In real terms, the C5 trunk measures 11.2 cubic feet in top-down mode, 13.9 with roof unfolded and in place. If you still don't get it, try to imagine two bags of golf clubs nestled in there; that's what

CONTINUED ON PAGE 111

When the top is up the 1998 convertible only loses 0.20 inches of headroom compared to the C5 coupe. The manual folding top is available in black or tan twill or white vinyl fabric.

CORVETTE AGAIN SETS THE PACE

Two weeks and a few days before the press was notified that the 1998 Corvette had won *Motor Trend's* Car of the Year award, word had broken of an equally prestigious honor for Chevrolet. On November 6, 1997, at the annual Specialty Equipment Market Association meeting in Las Vegas, Chevrolet General Manager John Middlebrook teamed up with Mary Hulman George of the Indianapolis Motor Speedway to announce that the new C5 convertible had been chosen as the pace car for the 82nd running of the Indianapolis 500, to be held May 24, 1998.

No stranger to the "Brickyard," Chevrolet has now been picked to pace the field at Indy 11 times, more than any other manufacturer. This year will mark the fourth such honor for the Corvette, with past appearances taking place in 1978, 1986, and 1995. A Fleetmaster convertible in 1948 was the first Chevy to pace the 500, followed by a Bel Air in 1955. Camaros did the trick in 1967, 1969, 1982, and 1993, and a Beretta convertible led the way in 1990. On 8 of the previous 10 occasions, Chevrolet has offered at least some kind of special commemoration, either an all-out limited-edition replica or a simple decal and paint package. Nineteen ninety-eight will be no exception.

In 1978 Chevrolet built 6,502 Indy pace car replicas (after originally planning a "limited-edition" production run of about 300) with a base price of $13,653.21, compared to the 25th Anniversary coupe's $9,351.89 sticker. A long list of "standard" options for these red-pinstriped, black-on-silver fastbacks included aluminum wheels, a front-air dam and rear spoiler, tilt-telescopic steering wheel, and all power goodies.

All of the Corvette convertibles that returned to the Corvette line-up in 1986 were actually designated as Indy pace replicas as owners could add a commemorative decal. It was their choice.

Nine years later, Chevrolet did get the limited-edition thing right with a tidy run of a mere 527 pace car convertibles, all done in Dark Purple and Arctic White splashed with some serious graphics. Price for the eye-popping Z4Z package in 1995 was $2,816.

Sometime early in 1998, Chevrolet will begin sale of its fourth Corvette Indy 500 pace car replica, and this publicity-seeking convertible will not be shy about grabbing the limelight. As always the goal was to stand out.

"The '98 Corvette Indy Pace Car should certainly fill the bill," explained Middlebrook. "We told the designers we wanted something that would grab people immediately, and they didn't disappoint us."

Except for the strobe lights specially fitted into a special tonneau cover on the real thing, the replicas will be identical to the actual pace car, mechanically as well as visually. The 345-horse LS1 V-8 needs no modifications to keep the pace at Indy.

All 1998 Indy Pace Car replicas will be painted a glowing Radar Blue accented by mostly yellow glaring graphics down each side, these culminating in a checkered flag flowing up over the rear wheels toward the deck lid. Yellow stripes will also run down the hood, and the inserts for the black leather seats will be yellow as well. And if that's not enough, the unique "in-your-face wheels" (Chevrolet press release words) will be done in shocking yellow, too.

Scheduled to drive the Corvette pace car on the track next May is professional golfer Greg "The Shark" Norman, who has been a spokesperson for Chevy trucks since 1995. "Of everything I've attempted to accomplish in my life, pacing the Indy 500 is going to rank right up there," said Norman at the SEMA event last November. "It's a once-in-a-lifetime opportunity. Approaching the 18th green in a major tournament is exciting—but leading a pack of roaring horsepower in that new Corvette convertible—that's going to be a special moment."

Only a lucky few will be able to share in that moment. Chevrolet plans to build only 1,158 pace car replicas, 53 of those for import. The 1998 Z4Z Pace Car Package (with automatic) will add $5,039 to the C5 convertible manufacturer's suggested retail price (including destination charges) of $44,990. Along with those leather sport bucket seats, the package will include electronic dual-zone heating and air conditioning, Theft Lock, a digital clock, a Delco AM/FM radio/CD player (with automatic tone control, speed-compensated volume control, and Bose speakers), memory package, and floor mats. The new-for-1998 JL4 Active Handling system, a $500 option for 1998 coupes, will also be thrown in as part of the Z4Z option. Installing the six-speed manual in place of the no-charge 4L60-E four-speed automatic will add $815 to the bottom line.

Let the race begin.

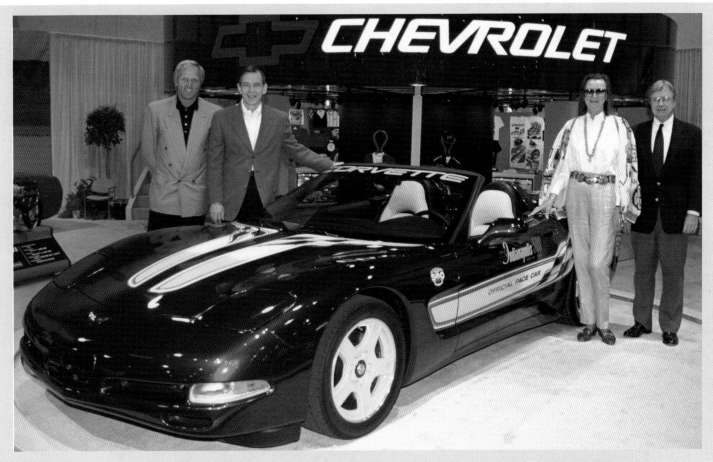

Chevrolet's new Corvette convertible was chosen as the prestigious pace car for the 82nd running of the Indianapolis 500 in May 1998. More than 1,000 replicas will be sold to the public. Appearing here, from left to right, are pro golfer Greg Norman, who will drive the pacer on race day, Chevrolet General Manager John Middlebrook, Mary H. George, Indianapolis Motor Speedway chairman of the board, and Leo Mehl, Indianapolis Motor Speedway vice president and executive director of the Indy Racing League.

The C5 convertible is both lighter (by about 100 pounds) and less expensive ($635 less) than its C4 predecessor of 1996.

anyone who has read a magazine review of the C5 convertible in 1998 is now doing.

Those eager readers might also be marveling at the C5 convertible's base price: $44,990, $635 less than the last C4 convertible in 1996. With the 1998 coupe's base sticker held at $38,060, the new convertible's price represents an 18.2-percent price jump from the coupe. Compare that to the 1996 convertible, which was priced 21 percent higher than the coupe that year.

That comparison becomes even more dramatic when you consider that the C5 price includes more than $1,300 in additional premium standard equipment, neat stuff like speed-sensitive steering, the run-flats' tire-pressure monitoring system, a mondo Bose stereo system, and a driver's power seat. Whether or not you think that's a lot for the money all depends on how much that 45 grand now burning a hole in your pocket means to you.

Chevy General Manager John Middlebrook thinks it's a real deal. "Value is Chevrolet's heritage," he said. "The Corvette has always offered incredible value when you compare it to its major competition. By beating the 1996 price and adding more standard equipment, there just isn't a comparable value available on the market. In addition to the price, the new 'Vette is a better car in every category. In many ways, the Corvette epitomizes value in its performance class."

Chevrolet decision makers feel the droptop Corvette is such a value they have reportedly geared up the Bowling Green assembly line to make 45 percent of this year's run convertibles. Corvette watchers haven't seen that close of a coupe/convertible balance since 1969.

New options can also become a part of the 1998 Corvette's value, convertible or coupe. An optional magnesium wheel, originally designed for 1997 export models and supplied by Speedline in Italy, has made its way onto the C5 equipment list for 1998. This bronze-tone, lightweight wheel saves 8 pounds compared to the stock unit. But that weight-saving comes at a price. The magnesium wheel option is presently priced at a very valuable $3,000.

More down-to-earth is the new-for-1998 JL4 option, or the active handling chassis control system. Active handling uses a system of sensors to read steering inputs, yaw rates, and lateral g-forces to better stabilize the car in emergency situations by selectively activating either the ABS brakes or traction control gear. Understeer or oversteer, it doesn't matter; the system will instantly command an individual wheel—inside or out, back or front—to brake or grip more precisely. Called "Bondurant-in-a-box" (in reference to former race driver and driving school guru Bob Bondurant) by *Sports Car International*, the well-received active handling equipment is priced at $500. Although experienced hot-shoes may want to pass on JL4 (it can be modulated to work without rear-wheel oversteer control), the rest of us will greatly appreciate the wonderful way this rookie-friendly hardware helps keep everything dirty side down. Active suspension is just one more reason to believe this is the best Corvette yet.

Beefs about the C5 convertible are almost too insignificant to mention. "If there's one complaint I've heard, it's that you can't find one to buy," said *Corvette Quarterly*'s Wes Raynal. And that's not a bad thing, at least not from Chevy's perspective.

As always, looks remain the easiest target. "It's a terrific car," began Paul Zazarine of *Corvette Fever*, "but it still lacks soul. Don't tell me I can put two golf bags in the trunk. I don't want to hear it."

"A few staffers thought the topless mode exaggerated the large-rump aspects of the C5's styling," wrote Csaba Csere. "Others thought that the bulges behind each headrest could also be bigger. Still, the overall look is rather stunning."

David Hill feels the same way. About the whole car. "The C5 convertible proves it is possible to marry high performance with top-down freedom," he said. "Simply put, this thing is incredible. Even more than the coupe, it will far exceed people's expectations. It even exceeded mine."

So what you're telling us, Dave, is that the 1998 convertible is the best 'Vette yet, no? We're having a hard time remembering which best 'Vette is which. You seem to be saying that so much these days.

CHAPTER SIX

INTO THE CRYSTAL BALL
What's Ahead for the C5

The C5 Corvette has been on the road for a year now, and it's still making news, some great, some not-so-great, all worth watching. Like any new car—as if a Corvette could be just "any new car"—Chevrolet's latest generation two-seater has had its teething problems. After waiting oh-so-long for those red-hot C5 hardtops, owners and owners-to-be alike learned in early March 1997 that GM was recalling the first 1,400 cars off the line due to the fact that a parts supplier had not properly heat treated a rear-suspension toe link, an oversight that might've led to that component's tragic failure at high speeds. That was the worst of the not-so-great stuff.

Other less threatening, yet pesky, items still qualified as not-that-good. Door glass sealing at high speeds was a pervasive problem in the coupe in 1997, and some early convertibles also allowed in a lot of wind noise around their windows. Complaints of too much under-hood noise, a not-so-sweet exhaust note, a buzz in the manual trans shifter, various electronic snafus, and door-panel degradation were also heard. Some had problems with the F45 adjustable suspension working as advertised.

Motor Trend editor C. Van Tune was alarmed over the way the rear-mounted automatic transmission, in cahoots with the frame's tunneled center-section, transfers way too much heat into the people compartments in heavy traffic and after prolonged operation. And he should know; he did that "Route 66" long-distance drive thing, tracing much the same route followed by 20 1998 convertibles in

The Corvette became a two-model family again in 1998 with the convertible's return. A third model, a first for America's sports car, is scheduled to appear soon.

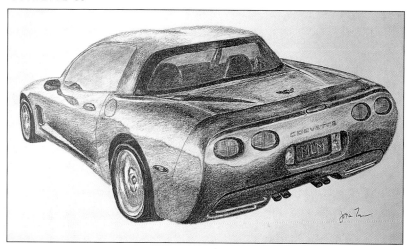

That third model will be a lower-priced "notchback" coupe with a fixed roof and a trunk like the convertible. Reports say this 1999 Corvette will be introduced at Indianapolis in May 1998. *Joyce Tucker drawing*

September 1997 as part of a Chevrolet promotional push for the National Kidney Foundation. Like so many others, Van Tune still can't say enough about the C5's performance after 1,700 miles in a Light Pewter Metallic (a new 1998 color) convertible. But his one complaint left him a little steamed. "The trunk gets so hot it turns your clothes into a wrinkled heap after a long drive," he said in 1998. "Drop in a frozen steak in St. Louis, and you'll have a fine roast by Tulsa."

On the flip side, C. Van Tune was also compassionate. "This first year has had build problems, like most new cars. Like the '63 did. Like the '68 did. Most problems have been fixed now, I think."

That they have. Along with those additional paint choices (Medium Purple Pearl Metallic is the other), new-for-1998 features include revised shifter bushings (no more buzz), an exhaust system retuned "for less noise and more music," window frame clips designed to keep the glass from sucking outward at high speeds, a reworked fuel pump that doesn't whine, a quieter accessory drive, and a half-degree more caster in the front suspension for enhanced steering stability.

The adjustable suspension option problem was also addressed. As *Car and Driver*'s Csaba Csere explained it, "apparently, the F45 suspension was calibrated on development cars fitted with prototypes of the Goodyear Eagle F1 GS EMT tires. Unfortunately, the production tires had different properties that were not well matched with the suspension. Recalibration in 1998 apparently solved that problem."

On the negative side of the ledger, one major deletion was made. In November 1997 it was announced that those $3,000 Speedline magnesium wheels would not make it onto the 1998 options list as had been promised earlier. According to Chevrolet spokesman Tom Hoxie, this ultra-expensive option was dropped because Speedline—the same Italian firm that helps keep the Porsche 911 Turbo off the ground—was simply not able to supply enough wheels to meet the demand here in this country. Too many orders were being backlogged waiting for the rims to show up. Originally designed for export Corvettes in 1997, the magnesium wheel would continue rolling on in 1998 beneath C5 models headed overseas.

Other than that, essentially everything else about the 1998 Corvette was a direct carryover from 1997, leaving us all wondering about and waiting for the next big news break. What awaits the C5 Corvette down the road and around the bend?

In the immediate future is the long-awaited "notchback" coupe, Jim Perkins' "Billy Bob" Corvette. Reportedly, this third body style in the C5 line-up will be introduced as a 1999 model in May 1998 at Indianapolis. Fitted with a trunk like the convertible, it will be stripped of various standard pieces to hopefully help bring its base price down close to the $30,000 ballpark. Most industry watchers doubt the true sticker will be that low. But regardless of its price, this bare-bones Corvette will weigh less and thus be naturally faster.

Rumor also has it that a hotter LS1 V-8 might be used in the coupe, if not in 1999, perhaps in 2000. Witnesses have reported mildly modified LS1 engines producing almost 400 horsepower on Powertrain Division dynos. Combine this much small-block muscle with that lightened coupe, and we may see ZR-1 levels of performance again—maybe even more. The 1997–1998 C5 is already so close to the old ZR-1 as we speak.

Reports that Chevrolet might even dust off that ZR-1 badge one more time (it was used in 1970–1972 and again in 1990–1995) have been heard, although that also appears doubtful. Much more believable is the prospect of a 400-horse C5 coupe being offered in factory racing trim. You tell us. All such speculation may well have been rendered moot by the time you read this.

So much for now. What about the long term? How many years will the C5 run?

Remember, the C4 rendition stuck with us through 13 model runs. Before that, the third-generation platform made 15 appearances. In this day and age, when the "what-have-you-done-for-me-lately?" attitude tends to prevail, such a long haul for this generation would surely doom the Corvette to that greatly exaggerated demise that repeated accounts have spoken too soon of for so many years now. Unless, that is, upgrades lie ahead somewhere along the way.

Veteran Corvette enthusiast Ray Quinlan feels the Corvette "will carry the C5 body, with some improvements, maybe as long as up to 2010."

"I have no crystal ball," added *Sports Car International* editor Randy Riggs, "but I do know we will live with the C5 for a long, long time. Obviously not as long as the C4, but it went on far too long for various reasons."

C. Van Tune predicts "maybe eight years for the basic platform." *Motor Trend*'s editor continued, "this isn't a car that will be revamped. The latest 'Vette will stay around awhile, and that's not a bad thing."

A rumor that surely qualifies as wild involved the possible revival of the 454 big-block V-8 as a Corvette power source. Twenty-four years after it last powered a Corvette, the 454 is still around as a Chevy C/K truck option, the L29 Vortec V-8. *Courtesy Chevrolet Motor Division, GM Corporation*

"I have no idea when you'll see another new Corvette," said Wes Raynal, editor of *Corvette Quarterly*. "This car could last them some time; they keep saying that this is it for awhile. But that also depends on what the competition does. How often will Porsche freshen its Boxster? Depending on things like that, we can probably expect a face-lift right after the millennium."

"I see a commitment to Corvette for several years," added *Corvette Fever*'s Paul Zazarine. "But I see no set deadline to go by for the future. It's hard to say exactly how long the C5 will run, but if you look at the length of the C3 and C4, they both got pretty long in the tooth."

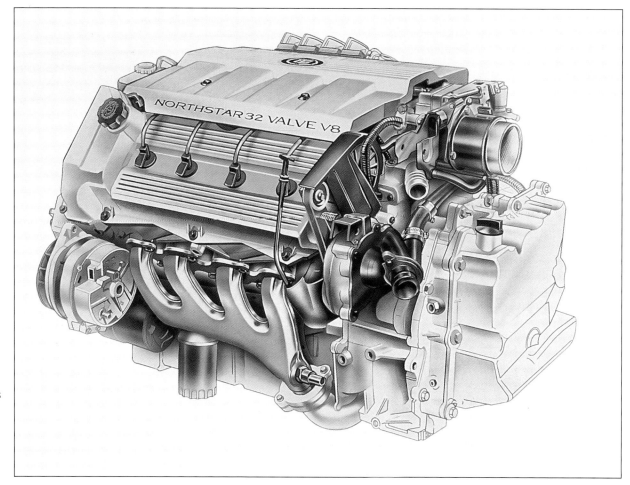

Many Corvette watchers have wondered about the possibility of Cadillac's 32-valve DOHC Northstar V-8 finding its way beneath a fiberglass hood. All reports say it would fit. *Courtesy Cadillac Division, GM Corporation*

According to Zazarine, the key to exactly how long the C5 sticks around—or even the Corvette itself for that matter—depends on what the Design staff does next. And he thinks they need to do something soon. "My personal feelings are that I think you will see a significant restyle very early in [the C5's] life, perhaps even by 2001 or 2002. Two-thousand-three is, of course, the 50th anniversary; by then all bets will be off. Who knows what they'll do."

An outspoken critic of the new Corvette look, as you might have already read, Zazarine feels a quick restyle will take place because, in his opinion, designers didn't quite get it right the first time. "Boy did we miss the boat here," he said. "Look at what Jaguar did with the XK8, what Porsche did with the Boxster. From the first day the [C5] design was locked in, it was already obsolete. Styling is the C5's weak point; it will be dated quite soon."

Right now, he feels Corvette is suffering slightly from a disappointed market. "Sales are a little behind what was expected," he continued, "but the '99 notchback coupe will inspire a little more excitement."

Corvette Brand Manager Dick Almond disagrees. Granted, the abbreviated 1997 number could mislead curbside critics—final coupe production for the first C5 was only 9,752. But he points to 1998 figures with confidence. Through December 1997, 1998 model-year production was 8,237. That translates into a 38.8 percent market-topping share of the high-sport segment. BMW Z3 was at 23.9 percent; Mercedes SLK, 11; and Porsche Boxster, 8.1. Price differentials aside, leading the league is still leading the league.

"We have our high seat again in that segment," added Almond. "I want us to be the big player in the high-sport market." Furthermore, extrapolating that early 1998 number puts the C5 right on course. "A production figure of 25,000 would be a good number for us," he concluded.

That number has long been a key to keeping the Corvette alive. But how many years will it continue on? Will there be a C6? "We see the Corvette in the future of Chevrolet for a long, long time," said Almond in January 1998.

If a long, long life does indeed await Corvette, how could another next-generation model possibly top the best 'Vette yet? An engine amidships maybe? All-wheel-drive perhaps? Smokin' sports cars from Porsche and Mitsubishi have in recent years eaten up the road with the latter feature. Concept Corvettes have demonstrated the former as far back as 1960 when Duntov's engineers showed off the CERV I.

Thirty years later, the popular CERV III concept car hit the auto show circuit with both, the latter and the former, inspiring more than one show-goer to greater expectations for Corvettes to come. "That concept vehicle was a handsome car that made a major styling statement yet still showed many Corvette vestiges," said Paul Zazarine. "I wanted to see more of CERV III in the C5 Corvette."

Will "more" be the answer? The Viper GTS coupe has 10 cylinders, 488 cubic inches, and 450 horses. Early C5 speculation (or was it wishful thinking?) by *Motor Trend*'s staff in 1994 spoke of Chevrolet possibly even reviving its old feared and revered 454 big-block V-8, a stump-pulling torque churn last seen beneath a fiberglass hood in 1974. Stranger things have happened. After all, the 454 is still hanging around the Powertrain Division as a Chevy truck option.

Or perhaps we'll see more tech. Powertrain engineers have milked the tried-and-true 16-valve pushrod layout for all its worth. How much is left inside the good ol' Chevy small-block remains to be seen. Certainly not much more, at least not with normal aspiration. Racer/car builder Reeves Callaway has never been shy about bolting twin turbos on his Corvette conversions, nor was Mitsubishi a few years back when it dazzled everyone with its 'Vette-eating 3000GT Spyder VR4. Both cost and complexity concerns will undoubtedly forever rule out any forced-induction tech.

As for advanced valvetrains, Chevrolet has already tried the 32-valve, DOHC trick before—and gotten burned. The ZR-1's all-aluminum LT5 V-8 certainly did deliver the high-tech goods—its four cams and four valves per cylinder were helping pump out 405 horses by the time the ZR-1 retired in 1995. But the LT5 also helped push the ZR-1 Corvette's price through the roof, well above, apparently, what a meat-and-potatoes American sports car buyer was willing to fork over. ZR-1 demand never did really materialize beyond that initial "I-gotta-be-the-first-on-my-block-to-have-one-up-on-blocks-in-my-garage" phenomenon.

Eagle-eyes will point out that David Hill did once wear a Cadillac engineering hat. And Cadillac does have that wonderful Northstar V-8 with four cams and 32 valves of its own. Yet another rumor has it that Hill made a point of engineering the C5's engine compartment with ample room for a V-8 configured exactly like the DOHC Northstar. Mere coincidence? We think not.

If this is true, the prospect of a "Northstar Corvette" would certainly be far less foreboding financially than the ZR-1 was during its doomed-from-the-start six-year run.

Rumors of a mid-engined Corvette go all the way back to the 1950s. Shown here is the mid-engined CERV I concept vehicle in 1960. This machine established some of the engineering baselines for the 1963 Sting Ray's independent rear suspension. *Courtesy Chevrolet Motor Division, GM Corporation*

Could another such high-tech Corvette catch on with consumers at a much more palatable price? And could Chevrolet engineers build it at that price? Would GM execs let them?

In addressing all those high-tech questions, consider this: Chevrolet is much more conscious of luxury taxes and corporate average fuel economy (CAFE) ratings than, say, Chrysler, whose Viper offers apologies to no one for depleting the world's oil supplies and filling Dodge's coffers. Anything at Chevrolet that threatens to radically reduce miles per gallon or radically raise a window sticker's bottom line will certainly rapidly rule out its inclusion in any future plans. Remember once more, Chevrolet is GM's price leader. And at the price, the C5 Corvette already offers more performance technology, as well as real performance, than any other sports car out there. Bar none. Translated, this means don't count on seeing any more all-new hardware for awhile.

"There won't be a radical redesign for the Corvette in the near future," said C. Van Tune. "There won't be a mid-engined 'Vette. There will never be a V10."

"I'm not wild about the mid-engined idea," added Wes Raynal. "The engine is practically in the middle of the car already. They've got the weight distribution down close to where they really want it, 50/50."

Beyond nuts and bolts, there's also the Corvette's identity to think about. GM's luxury leader and America's sports car have been mentioned in the same sentence before. Could the Corvette end up as the displaced flagship for a higher-placed GM division, say, as high as Cadillac? Although this discussion was suppos-edly squelched by Jim Perkins about half a decade ago, the Corvette never can seem to shake in-house jackals bent on killing it. Or curing it. Whether it needed it or not. Nor, seemingly, can it escape its oft-mentioned fate as a merged F-car/Y-car product.

Of combining Corvette and Camaro, this possibility remains nothing more than a rumor, and an apparently silly one at that. Reportedly, this talk, although loud and plentiful at times, never has come from the horse's mouth. "Those were outside rumors," said Dick Almond. "We would definitely never say that ourselves." According to Almond, Chevrolet has "absolutely no intentions" of ever combining the two. Or, as he told writer Don Sherman in 1996, "of downgrading the Corvette's hard-earned status as one of the world's finest ultra-performance sports cars."

"We will never see that happen, Corvette and Camaro joining; that would be a disaster," echoed Randy Riggs. "Corvette must keep a separate, distinctive position." As it is, by all accounts these days, it is the F-body platform that's in trouble, not Corvette. More than one source outside GM has predicted an end for the Camaro unless sales start turning around soon. To this rumor, Almond can only chuckle and refuse comment.

Of that "Cadillac Corvette" possibility, Almond was also adamant in 1996. "I, too, have heard the speculation that the Corvette is going to some other GM division," he told Sherman. "If I were Cadillac, I'd certainly want the car, but there are no such plans. I promise we'll fall on our swords before the Bow-Tie badge is replaced with a wreath-and-crest insignia."

So much for internal pressures.

Having to operate in the real world, Chevrolet's fiberglass fantasy also now faces all the same harsh realities that any other Chevy product does, something it didn't necessarily have to do in the past. A legend is still a legend, but it doesn't seem like all that long ago that the Corvette stood as an untouchable legend, this even with all those greatly exaggerated reports of an untimely death.

Porsche put another Corvette rival on the street in 1997, the stunning Boxster roadster. It's not anywhere near as powerful as the C5 Corvette, but it's not meant to be. It's more of a traditional sports car: small and sprightly. *Courtesy Porsche Cars of North America, Inc.*

Mitsubishi's 3000GT, with or without the all-wheel-drive VR4 option, stands as a major rival to the Corvette. In 1996 things really got hot when the Diamond Star guys let loose the 3000GT Spyder, a killer of a sports car with a retractable hardtop.

Nissan took its ball and went home in 1996, canceling its legendary Z-car, at least in the American market. Sales of the exciting 300ZX had dropped steadily through the 1990s. *Courtesy Nissan North America, Inc.*

BMW was the first of the high-level marques to get the entry-level, two-seat sports car ball rolling, introducing its Z3 roadster early in 1996. In six-cylinder form, it's now a real road rocket.

"Corvette has to make money now; it can't be just an image car," explained C. Van Tune. "And it will remain pretty much where it is until there is a major change in the marketplace."

Almost everyone asked agreed that the Corvette won't be going anywhere soon, but that, of course, hinges on what the customer wants. Or what he or she will take. People want high-sport machines like the Corvette; they can afford to buy them; they can afford to drive them; they can live with them in a workaday world; they simply love them—for now. Market pressures, however, can be fickle. And the Corvette is certainly not immune to having the bottom fall out.

"Corvette's future depends on what happens to the two-seat sport car market in the next few years,"

More competitively priced in Corvette's class than Mercedes' other topless two-seaters, the SLK debuted in 1997 as a 1998 model. A 191-horsepower, supercharged 2.3-liter four-cylinder was standard. *Courtesy Mercedes-Benz*

RIGHT: Mid America Designs' Mike Yager, the same guy who was presented with the last C4 Corvette at a ceremony at the National Corvette Museum in 1996, also managed to pick up the first C5 car delivered to the public. *Tom Glatch*

Talk of closing the Bowling Green assembly line or transforming it into a truck plant has been heard more than once over recent years. How much longer will this sign stand outside the Corvette's old Kentucky home? Only GM knows for sure.

said C. Van Tune. "Japan has already come and gone." Yet the departure from the American marketplace of sports cars like Nissan's long-respected Z-car has by no means rang a death knell for the high-sport segment itself. On the contrary, that action has only made life more profitable for Corvette. Things couldn't be any better.

"This is the greatest time in history for automobiles, for performance cars, for trucks, for sedans, for economy cars," added Van Tune. And it's certainly the greatest time in history for Corvette buyers. But for how long? "Who knows what will happen in the next five years or so," he continued. "Will government safety standards become too stringent? Will emissions standards go too high? If so, Corvette could grow too expensive. Chevrolet already learned that lesson with the ZR-1."

Concerning how far into the future the Corvette might prosper, Paul Zazarine could only guess. "A lot of things come to bear," he said, "sales, the economy, government involvement."

"If factors like these all grow too tight," chimed in C. Van Tune, "the Corvette will certainly go away."

Dick Almond agreed this time. "Everything we do has to do with the laws of the country or the laws of our buyers," he said. "If there is no high-sport market, if Ferrari isn't selling, if Porsche isn't selling and so on, then what good would it be if we were marketing a car that no one would buy?"

A little chilling, perhaps. But coldly true.

Fear not, however; the high-sport market does not appear even remotely on the verge of collapse. As for the Corvette, what do bystanders believe to be the best ways to keep better pace with that market in the future?

"I'd like to see it become a bit smaller," answered D. Randy Riggs. "I don't need room for two sets of golf clubs." Riggs also prefers more tech. "For a pushrod V-8, that engine is sensational. But I would like to see an overhead-valve V-8. Not like the ZR-1; that didn't work too well. I'd like to see something like the Cadillac Northstar."

Paul Zazarine's answer begins not with the car but with the men behind it. He doesn't feel confident about the Corvette's future as long as the powers that be are the powers that be. In his mind, it goes without saying that GM needs more "car people" in high places. "Chrysler is a vibrant company right now thanks to the men in charge 'with gasoline in their veins,'" he said. Additionally, Zazarine believes General Motors is running low on movers and shakers, men who cast long shadows like Zora Duntov, Bill Mitchell, and even Dave McLellan once did. "The last maverick left when Jim Perkins went out the door. We will never be able to go back to the old ways, but somewhere down the line, something will have to happen at GM."

But that's then, that's future stuff. For now, why not just enjoy the latest Corvette for what it is today? And that is . . . ?

"It's a terrific car," qualified Zazarine. "This is the first 'Vette that is feasible as your only car," answered C. Van Tune. "No sports car in the world can compete with it," added Ray Quinlan. "It's a great car, better than any Corvette ever built," replied D. Randy Riggs.

"The C5 is a helluva improvement over the old car," concluded Wes Raynal. "Its ride is remarkably better. It has that new appeal to a wider group of customers. It's more comfortable, easier to get in and out of, etc. And it is right in the hunt with anything else you can buy out there."

Sounds like the C5 Corvette, subjective slings and arrows aside, is a real winner overall. Got a problem with that?

INDEX